MW01132545

ROCK 'N' ROLL
IN ORANGE COUNTY

CHRIS EPTING

ROCK 'N' ROLL
IN ORANGE COUNTY

MUSIC, MADNESS AND MEMORIES

THE
History
PRESS

Published by The History Press
Charleston, SC 29403
www.historypress.net

First published 2014

ISBN 978-1-5402-1094-4

Library of Congress Control Number: 2014953184

CONTENTS

FOREWORD

L ike a lot of kids growing up in Orange County in the 1960s, I listened to the Beatles and the Rolling Stones and then a lot of things that my older sister brought home that were little bit different, like the Chambers Brothers. Plus, my dad was really into big bands, so I was exposed to that along with lots of other music. But in the early 1970s, I became a huge fan of Roxy music, bebop deluxe, mocked the bolt, David Bowie, Thin Lizzy—all of the hard-rock-meets-glam stuff.

I certainly was not what you would call a punk rocker or anybody who was angry and trying to change the world. I grew up just a mile away from the beach and enjoyed the really nice and standard-issue Orange County life in Huntington Beach. When my brother would bring home the New Music Express and I would read about all of the things happening in New York, like the Ramones and the Talking Heads, and then learn about the Sex Pistols over in the UK, I got very interested in learning to play music because of how simple everything seemed. I knew I couldn't play anything by Lynyrd Skynyrd or UFO or any of those things, but I sure could learn a Ramones song.

And that simple music, to me, resonated because it had heart, way more than anything that bands like Journey and Styx were doing.

At Edison High School, where I attended, there were a lot of kids in bands. One in particular was called Witchcraft, and it had this really pretty girl named Sandy West playing drums. Of course, she would eventually go on to play with the Runaways. The lead singer in Witchcraft was named Jim Decker, and he wound up being the singer in our band, the Crowd.

Witchcraft would play things by Black Sabbath, they would play the song "Born to Be Wild" and a lot of other cover songs, just like every other band in high school. But they also would play at house parties around Huntington Beach, and that's really what got my attention. I thought that just seemed such a cool thing—to stage concerts at people's houses.

As far as what the scene was like in Orange County back then for music, there really wasn't one. And none of us were coming at it from any real angry or political place. For me and a lot of other people, I think it was the connection to surfing, riding our bikes and skateboarding that really kind of set our tone.

So when we formed the band and Jim became our singer, we just wanted to do something a little bit different, just the logical progression of what he had already been doing in Witchcraft. We would go surfing in the morning and then start playing guitars during the day, and that became the logical step. All of the excitement that we felt from surfing and skateboarding started to get reflected in the music. The excitement we felt from catching a wave became the nondrug version of musical inspiration. We took all that intensity from things we would do during the day and simply channeled it into our music.

It was very common back in the late 1970s to have all of these house parties with kegs of beer and all of your friends around. That's just how people got together. There was no real element of danger and the worst thing that might happen would be the football player shows up and gets into a fight with somebody—just high school stuff. Guys might get in a fight, their friends all pull them apart and that's it. It wasn't like somebody would show up the next day with a gun and look for revenge. Once it was over, it was just over. If you got a black eye, it was no big deal. You just moved on. Today, it's a whole different situation.

We went to play a house party for this girl named Ginger Eastwood, who went to Marina High School in Huntington Beach. We put together seven original songs, and we played them each about three times to make up a full set. It was a great house party but to be honest, they were all pretty great back then. There was just a sense of community. Everybody you grew up with supported you. You might run into kids who went to different high schools at some of these parties or the cops might come break it up if there was a lot of beer there, but it was all good. It's just how we spent our time.

And we were just out to have fun. I was basically in a band to get chicks and play parties and not to change the world or anything really groundbreaking. This was not the Clash we are talking about. Now that said, throughout

Orange County, as it turned out, there were plenty of other punk bands that were coming from a living-on-the-edge philosophy and were trying to incorporate that sort of intensity in their music. But in Huntington Beach, that's just not how it was. I remember an interview some magazine did with our band, and one of our guys said that our dream was to live on boats in Newport Beach. That's not really punk. But we all laughed about it because that was honest. I wanted to surf and to skateboard and ride my Stingray bike in the dirt and hopefully make some money so I could have a good life.

Our drug was youthful energy, and we thrived on it. As we started to come together as a band, there really were no venues for a group of our caliber to play. We were very raw and inexperienced and had never even recorded anything. But we did play a lot of house parties and then started to get so popular that we eventually sort of grew out of them. This is before all social media, of course; everything had this underground flavor to it. But thankfully, once we outgrew our ability to play parties, we were lucky enough to land a gig at the Cuckoo's Nest in Costa Mesa. The owner of the place really didn't care for our music, but we did bring a lot of people in. That made a difference. If you can bring fans into a club, it will always have you back.

In retrospect, we didn't realize we were creating any sort of buzz with these huge house parties. But the house party scene really influenced a lot of other bands because it showed that you could actually draw a crowd even if you didn't have a ton of talent.

Our music is not like any kind of hard-core punk. I felt that we were always too pop for those who like punk and too punk for those who like pop. Just sort of stuck in the middle. What we were, exactly, was a rock band that just liked to play really fast music. We took the music we liked and just played it superfast. It was more or less just a joyous expression of what we heard on the radio.

Nobody was ever thinking about a scene or building up some sort of environment or legacy. It was all totally spontaneous.

So around this time, we were playing yet another house party, and a guy shows up from Posh Boy Records. He asks us if we want to record, which of course we do. And so a year later, a compilation called *Beach Blvd.* came out that included the Simpletones, the Crowd and Rik L Rik. And that became a groundbreaking thing for us.

Now all of a sudden we go from just playing house parties to being interviewed by Rodney Bingenheimer on KROQ radio in Los Angeles. We get hired to open up for the Cramps up in Los Angeles at the Whisky a Go Go, and Robert Hillburn from the *Los Angeles Times* actually reviews our set. We couldn't believe it. All of a sudden, it seemed as if we had broken through. All of a sudden, other bands were looking at us as some kind of trailblazers. We were all living proof of what could happen to a local beach band.

As for punk style back then, it was all do it yourself. It wasn't like you could go to the mall and buy a studded bracelet or anything. But that wasn't our style, anyway. Ours was much sillier. We would just spray paint our T-shirts and do things like that.

To this day, people still tell me how much they remember the *Beach Blvd.* record and how much it influenced them. Other bands like the Vandals looked at us and said hey, if they can do it, we can do it, too. They're just regular guys like us. And they were right.

Also, there was no segmentation back then when we would play clubs in Orange County. There was punk and rockabilly and all kinds of other music being played. It was really great in the late '70s, but then things started to get segmented and much more rigid in the early '80s. I also got kind of bummed out when the punk world became more dangerous in terms of concerts. The hard-core movement resulted in a lot of fighting and things that we were not into. We got into it to have fun, not to get into fights. As I started to become a better guitar player, I became more concerned with people connecting to my songs. It wasn't about a fashion statement, and it wasn't about violence. It became all about music for me.

And of course, we also got to see bands play, too. We were lucky to have the Golden Bear in Huntington Beach because we could see all of these new bands on the way up, and it didn't cost a lot of money. We could sit right against the stage. I remember sitting just a few feet away from the Talking Heads right before they became too popular.

I was so lucky to be in the eye of the storm seeing so many fantastic bands. People ask me now why didn't I document things back then, but you have to remember that I was just nineteen or twenty years old. I didn't think in those terms. I was too busy worrying whether a certain girl might've liked me to wonder about whether or not I should be taking pictures of other bands.

One of the best things about that time was the friends that I made. The guys that are in the Adolescents, we've been friends for thirty-five years now. A lot of the bands from that scene, when we all get together, it's like a high school reunion.

All of the groups, especially those that came out of that beach scene in the 1970s, are part of a real brotherhood. Some of the best friends I've ever made in my life are a direct result of being in a band back then, and we still all play shows together to this day.

As far as the local Orange County bands that really moved me back then, there are many, but two that really stand out are T.S.O.L. (True Sons of Liberty) and the Vandals.

Early T.S.O.L. in particular had such a different thing going for it. They were just a band that had to be dealt with. They had all of this substance and heaviness that really impressed me. There was just so much going on in their music. On the other side of the coin, the Vandals brought a goofiness to punk rock that I loved. It was very tongue-in-cheek, and they weren't trying to anger anybody but just kind of shock them with really stupid clothes and a craziness that was always amazing to me. They just had so much personality, still very intense, but they had a joy to them. Like I said, there were plenty of bands that blew me away back then, but those two in particular really had an effect on me.

As for memorable shows that we played back then, there are two specific moments that really stand out to me. One was really early in our career when we went down to Costa Mesa and made a deal to play at the Boys Club there. We just rented the hall after pleading our case at city hall and amazingly they let us do it. I'm not sure they really knew what kind of crowd we would attract. We promoted the show ourselves, and then that night, there were hundreds of people lined around the place. There were so many people we actually got nervous that maybe we'd oversold. Those shows were just so crazy and so crowded and really blew us away. It was different for us because that was the moment that we realized that what we were doing went beyond just backyard house parties. The kids that were there came from all over Orange County to hear our music. Those shows at the Boys Club were wake-up calls not just to us but to the fans, too. Something groundbreaking was really happening in Orange County.

The other moment I remember vividly that will always stand out was when the Crowd opened for the Ramones at the Rendezvous over in Garden Grove. It was in November 1979, and we could not believe we were actually playing with the Ramones. We felt like real hometown heroes that night, and all of our friends were there. A lot of people still talk about that concert as the first real punk show that they ever saw. It was a game changer for so many people, seeing one of the most famous punk bands up there along with this local band, us. I don't think we even got paid a hundred bucks for that, but it didn't matter. It was another big turning point in our lives. All of a sudden, we were not on the outside, but we were actually part of this thing, whatever you want to call it. It was happening not just in Orange County but all over the country.

I read lots of things today about punk bands in Orange County claiming to be the first this or the first that, and I try not to pay too much attention to it. Who's to say really who was the first punk band? But I do know this: there was no real scene before we started. There were no "punk" bands playing house parties all over the place. I take a lot of pride in the sense that we sort of helped ignite what was happening in Orange County. We have this song called "Love for Money" with these great lyrics our singer wrote that go "we took the fire that burns even brighter, young hearts of desire, we were the igniter."

That line says it all for me. I think we were like the igniter. It exploded past us, but I feel like we were the fuse on the powder keg. There was no master plan or anything, it was just circumstances. We never thought we'd open the door only to have a million people trampling right behind us. But it's cool. We still play music today. We didn't succumb to a lot of really negative forces back then. And we have some of the best memories in the world.

All thanks to that house party at Ginger Eastwood's house on June 20, 1978.

JIM KAA
Guitarist with the Crowd

ACKNOWLEDGEMENTS

With deep thanks to Bob Chatt, Bill Medley, Jim Washburn, Jim Kaa, Charles Epting (for shooting many of the wonderful photos), Ernie Grimm (for the incredible vintage punk flyers), the Sullivan family, Barry Rillera, Jordan West, Glen Byron, Tris Imboden, Chris (TK), Carole Babiracki, Robert Carvounas, Chris Andrada and, of course, my family for their patience and support. Thanks also to The History Press and editor Jerry Roberts.

INTRODUCTION

WITH JORDAN WEST

J ordan West has long been a part of the Orange County music scenes (among others). He arrived in the early 1980s, became a successful nightclub DJ, played drums in a few bands, was a roadie for a few more and then scored a gig with the famed KNAC.COM as an overnight DJ. He earned his nickname, the "Junkman," because of his love of collecting things at garage sales, used record stores and swap meets.

Long known as a musical tastemaker and shaker in Orange County, he shared some thoughts about his experiences here.

I was a DJ back in Orange County in the early '80s and wherever you went there was a live band or two. Every club in Orange County had live music, which was incredible. Even if it was a cover band, they still worked really hard and put on a good show. And some of these bands are still around. There was a band called Slingshot, and they still play around today in Orange County. This is like thirty years later! And obviously it wasn't just cover bands people went out to see. But man there was a lot of live music in Orange County, no matter what you wanted to hear. I worked a place called Faces in Huntington Beach that had been called Ichabod's during the 1970s. It was right on Beach and Ellis. What made them special was they had an after-hours license, so it was a place where kids could go really late into the night. And bands would get out of their other gigs and show up at Faces and jam late into the night. That was a big deal.

There was another place called Joshua's Parlour in Westminster, which later became the Marquee, and that was the premier heavy metal club from the mid- to late '80s. In the mid-'80s, they were getting bands before they really took off, and that's how I remember the Skid Row show. They had booked Skid Row right as they blew up, which was amazing. That was so lucky. Just as the album took off and hit number one was when they played the Marquee, and there were lines all around the place. All the hair bands played there, along with Jane's Addiction, L.A. Guns, Bango Tango, Little Caesar—just so many great bands played there.

Then obviously you had the Golden Bear, and there was also this place called Goodies in Fullerton, which was a great place to see a lot of alternative rock bands.

The Coach House obviously for a long time has been going great and has always been a great place to see bands. That place has been around forever now. The Cuckoo's Nest was sort of the ultimate punk and metal club back in the day. That's where Black Flag and so many other influential hardcore bands made the scene what it was. It was just the most authentic place. And then of course you had Radio City in Anaheim. I mean, U2 played there back in 1981. Can you imagine seeing U2 playing a club the size of your backyard? I drive by the site today, and it's hard to believe U2 was actually there.

That's where the band Great White kind of got its start, too, as I remember.

As far as what's always allowed the amazing growth of music in Orange County, everyone's got their own theory and I've got mine. I look at it like it's a bedroom community; every house has a garage, so there you have lots of places for bands to be created. Then you look at the fact that Orange County is made up primarily of families. So parents would help their kids out when they were starting bands. They would support them and get them the gear they needed and the lessons or whatever, and so you have this kind of structure that allowed a lot of bands to exist. Of course, there were a lot of other bands that were just rebels and got things done on their own. But generally speaking you did have a real support system of family and friends in Orange County, and you still do.

But then you also have the sense that bands, even when they got big, never really wanted to leave because they liked Orange County. It's a beautiful and comfortable place. So even when a band like Leatherwolf, who became one of the premier metal acts in the 1980s, when they got big they never really left Huntington Beach. They still hung out there and whenever they weren't touring that's where they hung out. There's just this sense of community throughout the county that I think has really contributed to all of the different music scenes over the years.

When I look back on the old days and compare it, I still see reasons to get excited today. The rebirth of venues like the Observatory to me is really exciting because they are so eclectic in their booking policy. That's kind of a throwback to how it was in the 1970s and '80s. You never knew some nights what you were going to get that was a really exciting feeling. You would get surprised by bands you've never heard of, and they would just change your life.

And while the music industry has changed a lot since then and there aren't as many venues for local bands to play live, it isn't like there is any less amount of great players and great writers and amazing young performers right here in Orange County. They're here. They just don't have as many places to play, so it's going to be tougher for them to get the word out. But it can still happen. You never know when you're going to get one of these resurgences, and then all of a sudden, a band like No Doubt explodes out of Orange County or more recently, Avenged Sevenfold.

When I first came to California, I thought all I was going to hear were bands like the Eagles and Linda Ronstadt. But when I arrived here in Orange County, I got slammed right away with the new wave scene, lots of hair metal and a whole lot of other things that I never expected. There are a lot of misconceptions about music in Orange County, but from what I've seen and learned over the years, it has long been a place for good music. Back in the 1960s, you could go down to Newport and watch Dick Dale. Then in the '70s, you had clubs like the Golden Bear where you can see all of your favorite bands. In the '80s and '90s into the '00s, all sorts of new bands sprang out of Orange County. I think back to the early days when Korn and Sublime were just starting out, and you almost couldn't believe your ears of just how good they were.

There's something very special here that results in a lot of cool musical history.

AUTHOR'S INTRODUCTION

As I sit down to write this, Orange County has just turned 125 years old. It will never get the respect that Los Angeles does when it comes to almost anything, but to truly know and understand Orange County is to not even let L.A. enter the equation. You see, Orange County easily stands on its own when it comes to many things, whether we're talking sports teams, restaurants or rugged countryside for some of the most beautiful beaches in the country.

And yes, it even boasts its own unique and definitive rock 'n' roll history.

That may be hard to imagine for those that did not grow up here, but talk to any kid that came of age during the late 1970s and early '80s—they'll describe to you one of the most dynamic and intense punk rock scenes that ever existed on this planet.

Go back about twenty years earlier, and you'll discover the impact that surf music had throughout Orange County, along with lots of folk, soul, blues and virtually every other genre of music that we tend to lump to the basic rock 'n' roll envelope.

Orange County is where Rickenbacker guitars were born and, soon after, where Leo Fender made a name for himself. It's where the Everly Brothers broke up and where Marvin Gaye performed his last concert. And stunningly, as you will soon learn within these pages, it is also the place where the seminal garage band classic "Louie Louie" was born.

This is where Elvis learned karate and Meatloaf first performed.

Author's Introduction

The history of rock 'n' roll in Orange County is a gloriously diverse tale of classic clubs, legendary bands and all of the usual myths and lore that seem to live so easily in the shadow of rock 'n' roll.

It is a story featuring some of the biggest names in history along with some of the more obscure characters that, while less famous, also play an important part in the tale.

The Orange County music scene to this day features lots of sex, drugs and rock 'n' roll. It has for decades, and it probably always will. You just have to know where to look for it.

It would be impossible to try to document every single band and venue that has existed in Orange County for the last sixty or so years. There simply is not enough space in this book. But I've tried to capture many of the highlights to help create as complete a picture as possible. That said, there is always room for more, and with the hope that perhaps someday there could be a second volume on this topic, I would encourage you to reach out to me with news stories and things I might've missed. Additionally, along with weaving in some exclusive interviews I conducted for this book, I have also included, as part of the narrative, a series of articles I've written as a journalist over the years.

So with that, let's put on our all-access passes and take a trip back in time to live and relive the many musical moments that have given this county much of its character.

Chapter 1

THE LATE 1940s–MID-1960s

C hronologically speaking, I suppose we could start this book back in
1932, when the Rickenbacker International Corporation, the electric
and bass guitar manufacturer, first started its operations in Santa Ana.
But I think we will save that for later. After all, those gorgeous guitars
that would go on to heavily influence the Beatles' sound would not be
designed for decades. In fact, until rock 'n' roll became popular in the
1950s, Rickenbacker specialized in steel guitars rather than the iconic
beauties that John Lennon would be cradling in the early 1960s. I mean,
who can forget seeing Lennon during the Beatles' famous 1964 debut on
the *Ed Sullivan Show* holding his Rickenbacker 325 Capri?

But again, we will get back to Rickenbacker later in our story.

It would probably make the most sense to begin this book with the story
of a highly imaginative dreamer named Clarence Leonidas Fender. Born
in 1909 to Clarence Fender and Harriet Wood, who owned orange groves
between Anaheim and Fullerton, "Leo" as he was called was something
of an electronics whiz as a child. At thirteen years old, after visiting his
uncle's automotive-electric shop, he became mesmerized by the loud music
emanating from the speaker of a radio that his uncle had built from scratch.

Leo Fender graduated from Fullerton Union High School in 1928 and
was studying to be an accountant while continuing to tinker and develop his
fascination with electronics.

In 1928, while working as a delivery man for an ice company in
Anaheim, Fender was approached by a Southern California band leader

who requested that he build a public address system that could be used for dances held up in Hollywood. Fender wound up designing and building six of these PA systems.

Fender married a woman name Esther Klosky in 1934 and then took a job as an accountant in San Luis Obispo working for the California Highway Patrol. He was let go due to the Great Depression and wound up back in Fullerton, where he opened his own radio repair shop called simply Fender's Radio Service in 1938 (after borrowing $600). Once word of his reputation got around, musicians and bandleaders began hiring him to build more PA systems, which he would then turn around and rent.

It was an interesting time in the music business. Amplified acoustic guitars were beginning to gain popularity, and so soon after, Fender joined forces with Clayton Orr "Doc" Kaufman, an inventor and lap steel guitar player formerly employed by Rickenbacker. Together, Fender and Kaufman, after forming the K and F Manufacturing Corporation, began designing and building amplified Hawaiian guitars and amplifiers.

In 1944, the pair patented a lap steel guitar with an electric pickup that had already been patented by Fender. One year later, they began marketing the guitar in a kit with an amplifier designed by Fender.

Noticing that the big band era was beginning to wane toward the end of World War II, Fender understood that the next wave of music would be based around small combos playing boogie-woogie, rhythm and blues, honky-tonk and western swing, among other styles. Within these combos, guitar players automatically embraced the new electric models because of the power they delivered. All of a sudden, one electric guitar player could provide all the power and verve of an entire horn section. Fender implicitly understood that an electric guitar, which was easy to hold and play, could have a profound effect on the industry.

In 1945, once Fender had begun manufacturing and selling guitars, he realized that he needed more retail space. The small storefront at 107 South Harbor Fullerton, where Fender's Radio Service was located, simply became too small. In 1946, he built two makeshift metal buildings in the 100 block of South Pomona Avenue in Fullerton. Soon after, he added a large brick building to his complex.

In 1949, he created the prototype for a thin solid-body electric model. One year later, it would be released as the Fender Esquire, a solid-body guitar with a single pickup. One year after that, the Esquire was rechristened the Broadcaster, and then soon after that, it became known as the Telecaster. Originally equipped with two single-coil pickups, it was almost instantly

Leo Fender. *Author's collection.*

embraced by country and western players, thus making it one of the most popular guitars in history. By 1950, the first "Fender Fine Line Electric Instruments" were being produced at the factory complex on South Pomona. It was here that the first telecaster, Stratocaster and Precision Bass were made.

For the next forty years, Leo Fender revolutionized the industry and kept Fullerton on the musical map. Today, the buildings where Fender worked, for the most part, no longer exist. There is a parking lot near the train station were the factory once stood. A small plaque affixed to the parking structure in a pair of murals pays tribute to the legendary guitar maker whose instruments are revered by the most influential and important musicians in the world.

The building where Fender's Radio Service was once located was recently nominated for placement on the National Register of Historic Places. The nomination text, which provides a solid yet succinct overview of Fender Guitars' history, reads:

Fender's Radio Service is being nominated to the National Register of Historic Places under Criteria A and B at the local level of significance in the areas of performing arts and entertainment/recreation. Under Criterion B, the radio store is closely associated with guitar legend Clarence Leo Fender, and under Criterion A, it is associated with the revolutionary basses, guitars, and amplifiers that he designed and manufactured. Aside from President Richard M. Nixon, no other individual from Orange County,

23

The Fender mural in the parking structure stands where the Fender guitar factory used to be. *Author's collection.*

A plaque at the site of the former Fender guitar factory in Fullerton. *Author's collection.*

THE LATE 1940s–MID-1960s

California, has had so profound an effect on the world as Fender. While there has always been disagreement over who invented the first solid-body guitar, there has never been any question that it was Fender, with his designs for affordable, easily mass-produced guitars, which facilitated the transition in popular music from big bands to small, guitar-driven groups. The instruments that he invented dominated and shaped popular music of the latter half of the twentieth century, music that was often at the forefront of social and political change, and more recently, has gone on to revolutionize the sound of African style and other world music. His amplifiers set the gold standard for reliability against which all amps are judged to this day. From the humble beginning at this radio store in downtown Fullerton in the mid-1940s, Fender was able to become one of the most radical guitar makers of the 1950s and 1960s.

He shook up an industry with his boldly styled amplifiers and instruments that changed the way in which guitars were produced and marketed, subsequently altering the way the world heard, played, and composed music. It was at this location that Fender designed his first solid-body electric guitars, and started the laboratory, manufacturing, and marketing processes and strategies that would serve him throughout the rest of his career. This early work done by Fender forged a new path for the inventor, and his innovations during this pioneering period—ridiculed by industry insiders—improved the range, durability, and affordability of amplifiers and guitars forever, while also allowing his company in the 1960s to set the standard for quality in the industry. Beginning in 1945, Fender started proudly putting Fullerton, California on every product produced by his then small manufacturing company, and that decision put the still small town of Fullerton on the map. Guitar aficionados still come to Fullerton looking for Fender's guitar business.

In the early 1950s, while Leo Fender was making history in Fullerton, over in Santa Ana a soon-to-be-legendary musical family had also begun finding their way into the business. Today, it's an industrial park, but back then, there was a house at 410 East Second Street where the Rillera family lived. Within that house, three brothers—Barry (guitar), Rick (guitar) and Butch (drums)—all took up instruments after being raised in a musical household. By 1955, they had formed what was likely the very first rock band in Orange County.

Calling themselves the Rhythm Rockers, they were influenced by everything they heard around them; music played by their father, on the

The Rhythm Rockers featuring Barry Rillera (third from left). *Author's collection.*

radio, in back rooms, dance halls—wherever it happened to come from, the brothers absorbed it and spun it into their own early brand of rootsy Southern California rock 'n' roll. Blending soul, R&B, Chicano, Latin, jazz and more, the Rhythm Rockers were at once the most innovative and flexible band in the county, able to play any kind of party or concert and always pleasing the crowd.

Glued to the radio, they would listen to DJ Hunter Hancock, who had radio shows on stations KPOP and KDAY. Rick and his sister Nancy began pooling their money so that they could invest in all the latest records by B.B. King, Memphis Slim, Percy Mayfield and many others. Rick also owned one of the very first Fender electric basses.

As David Reyes and Tom Waldman wrote about the Rilleras in their book, *Land of a Thousand Dances*:

> *The idea of a Rillera brothers band took shape in the pre-R&B era; by the time the group actually started, R&B had begun to make a major impact on urban black music, as well as the white, black, and Chicano audience. Barry and Rick became enthusiastic fans, and they listened to Hunter Hancock's show to learn the latest R&B songs. Their musical direction shifted slightly from exclusively blues to blues and R&B; the name Rhythm Rockers, coined by the piano player, implied a bigger beat than is common to the blues. However, they were not finished adding musical styles to the mix. The third ingredient, Latin jazz, came about as a result of the influence of their Mexican mother, many nights spent listening to Chico Sesma's radio program, and exposure to the Chicano*

R&B/jazz bands that were performing around Southern California. "The Chicano bands that played car clubs [social gatherings for Chicano teenagers and young adults] *all played R&B and Latin music,"* said Barry. *"We did, too." This was an unplanned, but not unwelcome, musical addition. "When I started this group, I didn't go with the idea of having a Latin sound," said Rick. As the brothers became more and more devoted to Latin jazz, especially the music of Tito Puente and Rene Touzet, they brought new members into the band, again with the intent of producing an authentic sound. At one point the Rhythm Rockers included, along with guitar, bass, vocals, and drums, three saxophonists, three trumpet players, a guy playing the timbales, and another guy playing the congas.*

The Rhythm Rockers had regular gigs up at Will Rogers Park in South Los Angeles as well as at many car club parties and weddings throughout Southern California. They also became the house band of sorts at Anaheim's Harmony Park Ballroom.

Anaheim's Harmony Park Ballroom back when it was called the German Concordia Club in the 1930s. This is where the song "Louie Louie" would be composed in the 1950s by Richard Berry. *Author's collection.*

R&B singer and songwriter Richard Berry wrote "Louie Louie." *Author's collection.*

Originally called the German Concordia club after being built in 1922, by the early 1940s, the building had been renamed and was a popular spot for social dances and concerts through the 1950s and '60s. In 1949, it even became the site of a popular country western TV/radio show called *Hometown Jamboree*, which was broadcast over radio station KXLA five days a week. On Saturdays, it aired over KCOP, Channel 13, in Los Angeles at 7:30 p.m. until going off the air in 1954.

A classic song was born at the Harmony Park ballroom in 1955 on a night when the Rhythm Rockers were playing there. Richard Berry, a black rhythm and blues singer from Los Angeles, would occasionally travel down to Orange County to sing with the Rhythm Rockers. On one particular night, he performed a song with the band called "El Loco Cha-Cha." It was originally called "Amarren Al Loco" (tie up the crazy guy) by Cuban bandleader Rosendo Ruiz Jr., but it became better known as "El Loco Cha-Cha" after a new arrangement by René Touzet, a Cuban-born composer and bandleader.

Inspired by the tune's infectious and simple rhythm, Berry went backstage after performing the song with the Rhythm Rockers and, while waiting to go back up and sing, decided to finish up a song that he had been writing. He would soon record a version of it but it wasn't until another band, the Kingsman, covered Berry's song that much of the world would first become aware of "Louie, Louie."

Barry Rillera, who still plays guitar around Orange County with his own band today, remembers the night well:

> *When I went backstage and Richard played me what he was working on, I kind of laughed. I mean, he basically just adapted part of "El Loco Cha-Cha" and turned it into "Louie Louie." That's fine, of course. A lot of songs are born after getting inspired by things that already exist. I just thought it was funny that he was so intrigued by what he just performed with us. And we just had no idea that night that what he created would go on to become such a rock 'n' roll classic. That's the first song every band would ever learn together in a garage.*

Rock journalist Dave Marsh wrote an entire book about the song called *Louie Louie: The History and Mythology of the World's Most Famous Rock 'n' Roll Song*. The *Publisher's Weekly* review is a testament to the staying power of the song:

> *In a vigorous discourse combining shrewd criticism and a conversational tone, Marsh (Glory Days) traces the evolution of one durable song from '50s cha-cha to '90s frat anthem. "Louie, Louie," in his estimation, is an archetype whose infectious "duh duh duh, duh duh" chorus bewitches teenage garage bands and major-label rockers alike. Inspired by a riff from Rene Touzet's "El Loco Cha Cha," "Louie" was written in 1956 by Richard Berry, who imagined a Jamaican sailor telling Louie, a bartender, that he's leaving to meet his girl ("Louie, Louie/Me gotta go"). "Louie" later achieved a cult following in the Pacific Northwest, and in 1963 a version by the Kingsmen became a national hit. Its slurred, indecipherable lyrics (the singer wore braces at the time) led to individual interpretations and an FBI obscenity investigation. Marsh closes the book on "Louie"—for now, anyway—with a lengthy discography listing "Louie" performers from Ike and Tina Turner to Frank Zappa to grunge band Nirvana. Crammed with trivia and wit, this text convincingly argues in mock-profound terms its thesis that "Louie" is a melodic phenomenon far bigger than the mere mortals who perform it.*

The modern-day site of where the rock 'n' roll classic "Louie, Louie" was written in 1955. *Author's collection.*

Like the site of the Rillera home, today where Louie Louie was born, there is an industrial park with no marker of any sort to claim the rock 'n' roll history that took place there. For Barry and his brothers, though, it would hardly be the last time they would brush up against history.

According to Bill Medley—who, with Bobby Hatfield, formed the Righteous Brothers—were it not for Barry Rillera, the Righteous Brothers may not even have existed.

Back in the early 1960s, Bobby, who had gone to Anaheim High School, had a group called the Variations, and I had a group called the Paramours. In a sense, we were like the only two real rock 'n' roll bands in Orange County. But that's really kind of relative. Because what Ricky Rillera and his brothers in the Rhythm Rockers were doing was sort of beyond where rock 'n' roll was at that point. They were just so ahead of their time. They were so revolutionary, I'm still not sure anybody knows just how influential they were and how they moved everything forward. They blended Hispanic music with rhythm and blues in a whole bunch of other ethnic influences that made them just the hottest band in the area. And so what happened was, Barry was playing guitar in both Bobby's group and in my group in between what he was doing with his brothers. They were just so legitimate, those guys. In fact, the very first time I sang on stage for real was when I

An early promotional shot of the Righteous Brothers. *Author's collection.*

got up to do a B.B. King song called "Sweet Little Angel" with the Rillera brothers. That's what showed me where I wanted my life to go. So anyway, Barry is working with both of our bands, and he told me all about Bobby and that we should try singing together, so we did.

After the Righteous Brothers were born, Rillera and his brothers would remain a fixture as part of their touring band for many years. As to how they received their name, it happened in 1962 during a Paramours gig when an audience member stood up and shouted, "That was righteous, brothers!" which prompted the two singers to adopt that name.

The Righteous Brothers first started playing at the Rendezvous Ballroom on the Balboa Peninsula in Newport Beach in the early 1960s. At one time, the Rendezvous had featured all the famous big bands, but by the late 1950s, the place had been shut down. That changed in 1959 when guitarist Dick Dale performed his first show there. The ballroom would soon become a hotbed of surf music, but it was also where the Righteous Brothers first connected with an Orange County audience.

As Bill Medley recalled:

> *Thank god our friend Mike Patterson convinced us to go down and play at the Rendezvous. It was just perfect for us, and the timing was right. We had just recorded a song that I wrote called "Little Latin Lupe Lu," which was about a girl I had gone to Santa Ana High School with. I'll never forget driving down to the Rendezvous with Bobby and hearing that song for the very first time on the radio. It was an out-of-body experience when that happened. Just unbelievable. Then all of a sudden, all the seventeen and eighteen-year-old kids at the Rendezvous went out and bought that record, and we were off and running. I remember when we were up there being inducted into the Rock and Roll Hall of Fame, I just thought back about how it felt hearing that record on the radio for the first time and how much it meant to us.*

The Rendezvous Ballroom was destroyed in a fire 1966. Today, at the site, there is a historic marker.

Looking back on growing up in Orange County, Medley fondly recalls what life was like 1940s and '50s:

> *Santa Ana back then was just like the '50s always look on television. We had all the malt joins, and it was kind of like paradise. When you see movies about the 1950s in America, that's really how it was around us, all of the good sides of it. It was total innocence, the perfect 1950s experience. And you had a great diversity of cultures, which many people don't realize. Santa Ana in particular was just an amazingly diverse place. For Bobby and me, growing up in Orange County, we were influenced by our neighborhoods but also by all of the great Los Angeles radio stations. You never forget the first time you heard Little Richard and Chuck Berry and all that kind of stuff. It was the black performers that really made us open our eyes. But for all those really famous influences that we got over the radio, I will always say that Barry Rillera is the person more people should know about. You have to remember, he was the guy that Jimi Hendrix was talking about when he said that the Righteous Brothers had a guitar player who was way ahead of his time. And it was his group, the Rhythm*

Rockers, that inspired the Chantays to form at Santa Ana High School in 1961. A year later they released their classic instrumental "Pipeline" and then would even tour with us a short while later. The Chantays are a great part of Orange County music history. But back to Barry, I can never forget what it was like being on that very first Beatles tour when George Harrison would come back to us to ask who was playing certain solos. He just couldn't believe what he was hearing backstage through the speakers. We would just tell him, it's Barry, and his jaw would drop. He just couldn't believe one person could be that innovative.

Rillera also has his own memories of being around the Beatles.

Paul McCartney sat down next to me on the plane and asked me how I got that sound out of the guitar. I explained to him how I bent the strings when I played, which nobody was really doing back then, and he said he was anxious to go explain what I was talking about to George. That first Beatles tour was a real experience for all of us. Often times, the kids in the audience were not aware that there were any opening acts before the Beatles. And so during many of our shows, all we could hear were kids screaming for John, Paul, George and Ringo.

And then there was that guitar sound that Rillera achieved, bending his notes by pushing up on the strings:

In many of the arenas where we played, the Beatles could sit backstage and here our set through a little speaker in their dressing room. I guess they liked the sound of my guitar that they would hear each night, and that's why Paul tracked me down on the plane. A few years later when I heard that beautiful George Harrison song, "While My Guitar Gently Weeps," and I heard him bending those strings, I remember smiling.

After that memorable tour, Rillera would go on to play hundreds of important recording sessions with producers such as Phil Spector, and he toured with Ray Charles and many other notable musicians. He was even performing the night of June 5, 1968, at the Ambassador Hotel in Los Angeles. That's the night Bobby Kennedy was shot in the same building. "That's one night that stands out to me more than any of the others. I remember all of the excitement in the building from all the Kennedy supporters. But then I remember the moment just after we all learned

A Beach Boys promo shot from the early 1960s. *Author's collection.*

what happened. Everything changed so quickly. It was just such a tragic night, and the way the mood turned is something I'll never forget." (On a side note, Roy Lee Ferrell, father of actor and Orange County native Will Ferrell, played organ and saxophone for the Righteous Brothers for about thirty years).

Back in Orange County in the early to mid-1960s, in addition to the rising popularity of the Righteous Brothers, there were many other musical breakthroughs happening as well.

The aforementioned Dick Dale and the Del-Tones were helping to invent surf culture at the Rendezvous Ballroom along with other surf acts, including the Bel Airs, the challengers and Eddie and the showman (who featured Dick Dodd, later of the Standells and "Dirty Water" fame). In late 1961, the Beach Boys had their first chart hit, "Surfin'"; a year later they released "Surfin' Safari."

There were a variety of other venues in Orange County that hosted surf bands back then, including the Chatterbox in Garden Grove and Retail Clerks Auditorium in Buena Park, where the Beach Boys played a memorable show in July 1963.

This early 1960s ad is from a show that took place at Retail Clerks Auditorium in Buena Park. *Author's collection.*

FRIDAY, OCT. 1ST

RETAIL·A·GO·GO

....PRESENTS

the MoJo Men

(STRAIGHT FROM 10 SMASH WEEKS
AT THE "CHATTERBOX" IN GARDEN GROVE)

The THINGS
The STYMEES
The LITTLE RASCALS

AGE LIMIT — 15 TO 19

Retail Clerks Auditorium
CORNER-STANTON & CRESCENT
BUENA PARK

In addition to Orange County becoming a hotbed of surf music and rhythm and blues, folk music had also taken root throughout the county. Clubs such as the Golden Bear in Huntington Beach (which would soon morph into a venue for many kinds of music), Cosmos and the Rouge et Noir in Seal Beach, the Paradox in Tustin, the Prison of Socrates on Balboa Island, the Mecca in Buena Park and the White Room (named after the famous Cream song) in Buena Park all featured many well-known and up-and-coming folk artists of the day.

Retail Clerks Auditorium in Buena Park was the scene of many surf music shows in the early 1960s. Van Halen also played here in 1977. *Author's collection.*

An ad for both the Cosmos folk club and the Prison of Socrates. *Author's collection.*

One of those artists was Tim Buckley, who attended Loara High School in Anaheim. After quitting the football team, he started focusing on music and, while in school, formed two groups, the Bohemians and the Harlequin 3. After graduating high school, he spent a scant two weeks at Fullerton College but then dropped out to devote himself completely to music. In 1965, *Cheetah* magazine designated Buckley a star on the rise, one of the "Orange County three," along with fellow folkies Steve Noonan and Jackson Browne.

Before dying from an overdose of heroin in 1975, Buckley built a career as a folk musician who also easily incorporated elements of jazz, funk, soul and avant-garde into his progressive sound. While Buckley never found big commercial success, other musicians' critics have long admired his innovation as both a player and a singer.

Another of the Orange County three, Steve Noonan, has had a respectable career as a singer-songwriter. But it was the last in the trio, Jackson Browne, who would go on to become one of the most well known an artistic success stories from Orange County.

Born Clyde J. Browne, he arrived in Fullerton at

Jackson Browne attended Sunny Hills High School in Fullerton. *Author's collection.*

age twelve and graduated from Sunny Hills High School in 1966 at age seventeen. He started writing songs a couple of years earlier and would spend time at the Paradox, a tiny coffeehouse in Tustin where he could see touring folk music stars in the flesh who no doubt inspired him. It was also at the Paradox where the Nitty-Gritty Dirt Band first attracted a following. Brown spent time in the band for a few months in 1966 before heading off to Los Angeles to launch what would soon become one of the most vaunted musical careers of his generation.

But it all started for him in Orange County, in a tiny little club where he could go see such performers as Jack Elliott, Sonny Terry, Hoyt Axton, Tim Buckley and even comedians like Steve Martin and Pat Paulsen.

Closer to the ocean, club owner Theodore "Ted" Nikas ran the Golden Bear, the Prison of Socrates, the Rouge et Noir and Cosmos in Seal Beach.

A tragic story that took place in 1966 is attached to the Cosmos club. The popular African American gospel folk duo Joe and Eddie (Joe Gilbert and Eddie Brown) had finished a show at the club on August 6. On the way

Back in the 1960s, this was the location of Cosmos folk club in Seal Beach. *Author's collection.*

The ruins of the Marina Palace in Seal Beach. *Author's collection.*

home, Gilbert was killed in a car accident. He left behind a wife and two sons, and Eddie Brown continued as a solo act.

Just a few blocks away from Cosmos was the Marina Palace, a converted Quonset Hut that in the mid- to late '60s hosted such headliners as Ike and Tina Turner, Stevie Wonder, Little Richard and then later in the '60s, the Seeds, Strawberry Alarm Clock and early appearances by Alice Cooper and Van Morrison, among other shows.

Opened originally by Bill Robertson as the Airport Club in 1950, it was a haven for gamblers who were drawn to the bingo and draw poker tables, which were then legal in California. Once those games were outlawed, the club went out of business, but it was soon reopened by Robertson. Renamed the Marina Palace in the early 1960s, the club was originally supposed to be the first of Bob Eubanks's Cinnamon Cinder clubs, but that never happened. In addition to big-name touring acts, many local bands like Hot Sauce and Things to Come regularly performed there. In 1974, the Marina Palace went out of business, though some of the ruins still remain today on Pacific Coast Highway in Seal Beach.

Starting in the 1940s, with Leo Fender and following up to the '60s with the birth of surf music, the Righteous Brothers, "Louie Louie" and a host of legendary clubs, Orange County was soon poised for the next chapter of its music history. And soon, concerts would start moving beyond just the clubs and into theaters and arenas. As well, one of the most famous rock festivals in history would happen in Orange County.

One particular venue that helped prove that Orange County could indeed support popular acts was the Melodyland Theater, which opened just across Harbor Boulevard from Disneyland in 1963. With a seating capacity of 3,200, Melodyland catered to an older crowd with popular performers such as Johnny Carson, Andy Devine, Jack Palance, Liza Minnelli and Bill Cosby. But it also hosted James Brown, the Dave Clark Five and other, somewhat more hip acts than the standard, middle-of-the-road pop and comedy performers.

There were other venues as well that helped solidify Orange County as a must-consider place to stop for some of the most famous rock 'n' roll acts in the world.

Before we get to those things, though, it's worth looking back at what started this chapter off: Rickenbacker guitars. As mentioned previously, it wasn't until the explosion of rock 'n' roll that the Santa Ana–based company really made a name for itself. It's impossible to know if Adolph Rickenbacker and George Beauchamp, the two men who founded the

An aerial view of the Melodyland Theater in Anaheim. *Author's collection.*

company in order to sell electrical whining guitars, could ever have imagined where that might lead.

Made in Orange County for their entire existence, Rickenbacker guitars gained popularity in the early 1960s after John Lennon purchased a Rickenbacker 325 Capri in Germany. He played the guitar on the *Ed Sullivan Show* when the Beatles made their debut in 1964 and then began collecting the guitars shortly after. George Harrison had also purchased a Rickenbacker during a brief visit to the United States in 1963 to visit his sister. A representative from Rickenbacker met with the band in New York City in February 1964 and gave Harrison a model 360/12, the second electric twelve-string built by Rickenbacker. This guitar became an essential part of the Beatles' sound on their *Hard Day's Night* album and many other Beatles tunes through late 1964. All of those Beatles guitars from 1964 on were manufactured in Orange County.

Some information from the Rickenbacker website:

> *Paul McCartney used a Hofner bass in the early years of Beatlemania but soon had a Fireglo twin-pickup Rick bass, an early Model 4001S with dot inlays and no bindings. Its features closely resembled those of the Rose, Morris Model 1999 later played and made even more famous by Chris*

Squire of Yes. These solid body basses—which seemed so modern in the 1960s—used horseshoe pickups in the bridge position, thus proving the validity of Beauchamp's original 1930s design. Good ideas are timeless.

While Paul's Rick bass surged like an undertow, George Harrison's double-bound 360/12 (the second one made by the company) defined a new tone at the other end of the audio spectrum. Its ringing sound embellished "You Can't Do That," "Eight Days a Week," and "A Hard Day's Night," to name just three 12-string cuts from the 1964–65 period. Thus the Beatles created unprecedented, international interest in Rickenbackers, which many fans actually believed came from Britain.

Soon, Rickenbackers created the sound and image of bands on both sides of the Atlantic. Jim (later Roger) McGuinn—who bought a Rickenbacker 360/12 after seeing the movie "A Hard Day's Night"—literally made the bell-like quality of its tone the foundation of the Byrds' early style. His later 3-pickup 370/12 featured custom wiring, but was still for the most part an off-the-rack instrument. The Who's Peter Townshend, Creedence Clearwater Revival's John Fogerty, Steppenwolf's John Kay, and many other well-known 1960s guitarists became faithful Rickenbacker users. What had been a six-week waiting period from the factory for some models became a six-month (or longer) waiting period in the mid 1960s.

This rapid growth in demand led to changes in the company. Before 1964 all Rickenbacker guitars had been made at the original Electro String factory in Los Angeles. That year Hall moved it over a six-month period to Santa Ana, in nearby Orange County. Despite the disruption in production during the transition, the new factory had increased production capacity. During this same period, the distributor Radio-Tele changed names to Rickenbacker, Inc., thus adopting a moniker people had used all along anyway.

Rickenbacker. Fender. "Louie, Louie." Righteous Brothers. Tim Buckley. Jackson Browne. All were homegrown in Orange County. The county was exporting a lot of talent around the world in many forms. Now it was time to import some.

Chapter 2

THE LATE 1960s–MID-1970s

O f all the music venues in Orange County, arguably the most beloved, historic and significant was the Golden Bear in Huntington Beach. The Golden Bear opened at 306 Pacific Coast Highway (just across from the pier) as a restaurant in the 1920s. Designed by renowned Southern California architect Ernest Ridenour, movie stars back then would motor down from Hollywood for dinner after a day at the beach. The original owner, Harry Bakre, retired in 1951. The business was home to various restaurants and then sat vacant for several years after Bakre's death in 1957.

Then, in 1963, Delbert Kauffman took over the club and established it as a folk venue. In the mid-'60s, Kauffman brought in a variety of diverse acts that represented the modern folk movement that was taking place. The very first act they hosted was a group called Les Baxter's Balladeers, which featured a young David Crosby. The Lovin' Spoonful, Hoyt Axton, Buffalo Springfield and many other bands would appear at the Golden Bear in the three years that Kaufman ran the place. (While it was rumored that Bob Dylan had played there, this is untrue. In fact what happened was that the Golden Bear promoted a concert where Dylan performed in nearby Long Beach at Wilson High School in December 1964.) But running a club proved too much of a financial challenge for Kaufman, and by 1966, he was bankrupt.

The Golden Bear closed again, but not for long. This is when the aforementioned George Nikas reopened the club in 1966 while also opening venues in nearby Seal Beach. With his guidance, the club continued to grow

A vintage ad from
the Golden Bear.
Author's collection.

and was soon booking more national acts, including the Flying Burrito Brothers, Richie Havens and Janis Joplin, who appeared many times at the club. Nikas would operate the club until 1974, further establishing it as one of the most popular and acclaimed venues in Southern California.

Chris Hillman, formally of the Byrds and the Flying Burrito Brothers, remembers the Golden Bear well:

> *What an amazing ambiance that place had. Warm and intimate. I had surfed at Huntington Beach once as a kid, being from San Diego and all, so that's all I knew about the city before I played there. But to appear at the Bear was always a treat. We'd get down there early, maybe four in the afternoon or so, to sound check. Then we'd all head out on the pier to that place at the end, it was like a coffee shop, and we'd have some of the best hamburgers I've ever eaten. That whole set up, the club, the pier, the ocean, it was magical.*

The exterior of the Golden Bear in Huntington Beach. *Author's collection.*

It was also a different vibe than playing in L.A. When the Beatles said we [the Byrds] were their favorite American band, it made us feel special, and we were treated like stars around town. But down at the Bear, it was more laid-back and cool, a great environment to play in—and the food there was great, too. Why does it always come back to the food, for me? It's harder and harder to find places that like. I remember being there with McGuinn, Clark and Hillman and Tom Petty came down to meet us and hang out. It was that kind of place. A great hangout—and you never knew who might show up.

Musician Marc Volman of the legendary Turtles played the Golden Bear many times and says it was a special place for the band. "We had great fan support there and the place was very professional. They paid market value for bands and filled an important void. For us it was always a good gig."

Just a couple doors away from the Golden Bear, two other venues opened around 1967. There was the basement club called the Salty Cellar (which also attracted name acts and featured a house band called the Blues Syndicate) and then a smaller club called Syndicate 3000. As burgeoning as the music scene was in the laid-back little surf town, there were other venues around the county that were beginning to attract attention by luring in both big-name an up-and-coming stars of Huntington Beach.

A 1982 advertisement for the Golden Bear. *Author's collection.*

Disneyland of all places had actually become a remarkably diverse musical venue by the mid-1960s. During the summer, there was a wildly active musical schedule that brought many popular acts to Orange County. The last year that the park featured primarily big-band music in its concert series that would kick off over Memorial Day weekend was 1965.

By 1966, folk, country and pop music all but ruled the performances at the Magic Kingdom during summer. On Monday evenings, Disneyland would feature the folk Hootenanny. Tuesday it was called a Humdinger and targeted a younger audience. Wednesdays were held for the Country Music Jubilee, and on Thursdays it was guest band night.

Reviewing the entire summer schedule, it is amazingly impressive the caliber of acts that Disneyland brought in during 1966. And it's impossible to gauge how much they helped grow the music industry by providing such easy access to so much talent.

June 20 (Monday) 9:00 a.m.–12:00 a.m. *Hootenanny*: the Womenfolk; David Troy; Dapper Dans; Bud and Len; Clara Ward Singers.

June 21 (Tuesday) 9:00 a.m.–12:00 a.m. *Humdinger*: Vic Dana; the Blossoms; H.B. Barnum; Tina Mason; the Mustangs; Humdinger Dancers; the Association.

June 22 (Wednesday) 9:00 a.m.–12:00 a.m. *Country Music Jubilee*: Roy Acuff; the Dillards; Kathy Taylor; Dorsey Burnett Band; the Association.

June 23 (Thursday) 9:00 a.m.–12:00 a.m. *Guest Band Nite*: the Association.

June 24 (Friday) 9:00 a.m.–1:00 a.m.: the Association.

June 25 (Saturday) 9:00 a.m.–1:00 a.m.: the Association.

June 27 (Monday) 9:00 a.m.–12:00 a.m. *Hootenanny*: Greenwood County Singers; Kathy Taylor; Tim Morgan; Ward Singers.

June 28 (Tuesday) 9:00 a.m.–12:00 a.m. *Humdinger*: Jackie DeShannon; Olympics; Bantams; Humdinger Dancers; Jim Doval and the Gauchos.

June 29 (Wednesday) 9:00 a.m.–12:00 a.m. *County Music Jubilee*: Roy Clark; Ramblers; Billy Armstrong; Jim Doval and the Gauchos.

June 30 (Thursday) 9:00 a.m.–12:00 a.m. *Guest Band Nite*: Jim Doval and the Gauchos.

July 1 (Friday) 9:00 a.m.–1:00 a.m.: Jim Doval and the Gauchos.

July 2 (Saturday) 9:00 a.m.–1:00 a.m.: Jim Doval and the Gauchos.

July 4 (Monday) 9:00 a.m.–12:00 a.m. *Hootenanny*: the Dillards; Steve Gillette; Darleen Carr; Candy Company; Dapper Dans; Bud and Len; Clara Ward Singers.

July 5 (Tuesday) 9:00 a.m.–12:00 a.m. *Humdinger*: Joey Paige; Ketty Lester; New Classic Singers; the Mustangs; Humdinger Dancers; the Spats.

July 6 (Wednesday) 9:00 a.m.–12:00 a.m. *Country Music Jubilee*: George Hamilton IV; Sue Thompson; the Spats.

July 7 (Thursday) 9:00 a.m.–12:00 a.m. *Guest Band Nite*: the Spats.

July 8 (Friday) 9 a.m.-1 a.m.: the Spats.

The Late 1960s–Mid-1970s

July 9 (Saturday) 9 a.m.-1 a.m.: the Spats.
July 11 (Monday) 9:00 a.m.–12:00 a.m. *Hootenanny*: the Pair Extraordinaire; the Aquamen; David Troy; Jim and Jean; Dapper Dans; Bud and Len; Clara Ward Singers.
July 12 (Tuesday) 9:00 a.m.–12:00 a.m. *Humdinger*: Leslie Gore; the Rivingtons; the Mustangs; Humdinger Dancers; Dobie Gray; the Sunrays.
July 13 (Wednesday) 9:00 a.m.–12:00 a.m. *Country Music Jubilee*: Minnie Pearl; the Sunrays.
July 14 (Thursday) 9:00 a.m.–12:00 a.m. *Guest Band Nite*: the Sunrays.
July 15 (Friday) 9:00 a.m.–1:00 a.m.: the Sunrays.
July 16 (Saturday) 9:00 a.m.–1:00 a.m.: the Sunrays.
July 18 (Monday) 9:00 a.m.–12:00 a.m. *Hootenanny*: Joe and Eddie; Irish Rovers; Mickey Elley; Disneyland Regulars; Clara Ward Singers.
July 19 (Tuesday) 9:00 a.m.–12:00 a.m. *Humdinger*: April and Nino; Jackie Lee; Gloria Jones; the Mustangs; Humdinger Dancers; the Regents.
July 20 (Wednesday) 9:00 a.m.–12:00 a.m. *Country Music Jubilee*: Hank Thompson; Wanda Jackson; the Regents.
July 21 (Thursday) 9:00 a.m.–12:00 a.m. *Guest Band Nite*: the Regents.
July 22 (Friday) 9:00 a.m.–1:00 a.m.: the Regents.
July 23 (Saturday) 9:00 a.m.–1:00 a.m.: the Regents.
July 25 (Monday) 9:00 a.m.–12:00 a.m. *Hootenanny*: Hoyt Axton; Goose Creek Symphonic Band & Stage Door Company; Disneyland Regulars.
July 26 (Tuesday) 9:00 a.m.–12:00 a.m. *Humdinger*: Brenda Holloway; Ray Peterson; the Steiner Bros.; the Mustangs; Humdinger Dancers; Dobie Gray; the Sounds of Soul.
July 27 (Wednesday) 9:00 a.m.–12:00 a.m. *Country Music Jubilee*: Canadian Sweethearts; Glen Campbell; the Sounds of Soul.
July 28 (Thursday) 9:00 a.m.–12:00 a.m. *Guest Band Nite*: the Sounds of Soul.
July 29 (Friday) 9:00 a.m.–12:00 a.m.: the Sounds of Soul.
July 30 (Saturday) 9:00 a.m.–12:00 a.m.: the Sounds of Soul.
August 1 (Monday) 9:00 a.m.–12:00 a.m. *Hootenanny*: the New Society; Walt Conley; the Uncalled Four.
August 2 (Tuesday) 9:00 a.m.–12:00 a.m. *Humdinger*: Mel Carter; the Standells; Carolyn Daye.
August 3 (Wednesday) 9:00 a.m.–12:00 a.m. *Country Music Jubilee*: Freddie Hart and His Band; Mary Taylor; Jerry Naylor.
August 4 (Thursday) 9:00 a.m.–12:00 a.m. *Guest Band Nite*: the Magnificent VII.

August 5 (Friday) 9:00 a.m.–1:00 a.m.: the Magnificent VII.

August 6 (Saturday) 9:00 a.m.–1:00 a.m.: the Magnificent VII.

August 8 (Monday) 9:00 a.m.–12:00 a.m. *Hootenanny*: Irish Rovers; David Troy; Darleen Carr; Dixson Bowles and the Dan Blocker Singers.

August 9 (Tuesday) 9:00 a.m.–12:00 a.m. *Humdinger*: the Hondells; Tina Mason.

August 10 (Wednesday) 9:00 a.m.–12:00 a.m. *Country Music Jubilee*: Tex Williams; Le Garde Twins; Cathie Taylor

August 11 (Thursday) 9:00 a.m.–12:00 a.m. *Guest Band Nite*: Knickerbockers.

August 12 (Friday) 9:00 a.m.–1:00 a.m.: Knickerbockers.

August 13 (Saturday) 9:00 a.m.–1:00 a.m.: Knickerbockers.

August 15 (Monday) 9:00 a.m.–12:00 a.m. *Hootenanny*: the Dillards; the New Folk Trio; Tim Morgon; Steve Gillette; Disneyland Regulars.

August 16 (Tuesday) 9:00 a.m.–12:00 a.m. *Humdinger*: Joey Paige; Gloria Jones; the Rivingtons; the Regents.

August 17 (Wednesday) 9:00 a.m.–12:00 a.m. *Country Music Jubilee*: Jimmy Wakely; Joe & Rose Lee Maphis; the Regents.

August 18 (Thursday) 9:00 a.m.–12:00 a.m. *Guest Band Nite*: the Regents.

August 19 (Friday) 9:00 a.m.–1:00 a.m.: the Regents.

August 20 (Saturday) 9:00 a.m.–1:00 a.m.: the Regents.

August 22 (Monday) 9:00 a.m.–12:00 a.m. *Hootenanny*: the Back Porch Majority; Aquamen; Fred Thompson; Disneyland Regulars.

August 23 (Tuesday) 9:00 a.m.–12:00 a.m. *Humdinger*: Bobby Sherman; the Two People; the Bantams; the Premiers.

August 24 (Wednesday) 9:00 a.m.–12:00 a.m. *Country Music Jubilee*: the Geezinslaw Brothers; Bob Morris; Faye Hardin; the Premiers.

August 25 (Thursday) 9:00 a.m.–12:00 a.m. *Guest Band Nite*: the Premiers.

August 26 (Friday) 9:00 a.m.–1:00 a.m.: the Premiers.

August 27 (Saturday) 9:00 a.m.–1:00 a.m.: the Premiers.

August 29 (Monday) 9:00 a.m.–12:00 a.m. *Hootenanny*: the Greenwood Singers; Casey Anderson; Goose Creek Symphonic Band & Stage Door Company; Disneyland Regulars.

August 30 (Tuesday) 9:00 a.m.–12:00 a.m. *Humdinger*: Martha and the Vandellas; the Mustangs; Humdinger Dancers; the Spats.

August 31 (Wednesday) 9:00 a.m.–12:00 a.m. *Country Music Jubilee*: Rex Allen Show; Jimmy Wallis; the Spats.

September 1 (Thursday) 9:00 a.m.–12:00 a.m. *Guest Band Nite*: the Spats.

September 2 (Friday) 9:00 a.m.–12:00 a.m.: the Spats.

September 3 (Saturday) 9:00 a.m.–1:00 a.m.: the Spats.

September 4 (Sunday) 9:00 a.m.–1:00 a.m.: the Spats; Nellie Lutcher.

THE LATE 1960s–MID-1970s

September 5 (Monday) 10:00 a.m.–12:00 a.m. *Hootenanny*: Disneyland Regulars.

September 7 (Wednesday) 10:00 a.m.–12:00 a.m. *Country Music Jubilee*: Merle Haggard; the Dillards; Bonnie Owens; Jimmy Wallis.

In the early 1970s, Disneyland would be the site of a monumental moment in rock history. But more will come on that later.

The music landscape in Orange County changed from August 3 to August 4, 1968. This is when the Newport Pop Festival came to the Orange County Fairgrounds in Costa Mesa. Not only was it the first concert ever to have more than 100,000 paid attendees, but it was also one of the first major music festivals ever to be held in Southern California.

Organized by twenty-six-year-old Gary Schmidt and his father, Al, the festival was originally set to be held inside the actual fairgrounds in an outdoor pavilion. But once everyone got a sense of how many people would be attending in the days leading up to the show, the decision was made to move the festival to the large adjoining parking lots. This meant that there would be no shade for attendees, and there was a mad scramble to move all the fencing, staging, sanitation and food concessions to the new area. As a result, things did not go as smoothly as originally planned.

But the lineup was incredibly impressive, and many fans today have fond memories of the festival.

On Saturday, August 3, performers included Alice Cooper, Canned Heat, the Chambers Brothers, Charles Lloyd Quartet, Country Joe and the Fish, the James Cotton Blues Band, the Paul Butterfield Blues Band, Sonny and Cher, Steppenwolf and Tiny Tim.

The Sunday, August 4 lineup included Blue Cheer, Eric Burdon and the Animals, the Grateful Dead, Illinois Speed Press, Iron Butterfly, Jefferson Airplane, Quicksilver Messenger Service, the Byrds and Things to Come.

Today, Gary Schmidt makes his home in Nevada. When asked what a few of his favorite memories were from that weekend, he offered, "Taking Marty Balin and Grace Slick in a ride over the event in the helicopter, gate control, Chamber Brothers and Eric Burdon. There is film available online now. My photos burned up in an album in a house fire, but I still have the negatives somewhere but have not found them yet."

This was how the event was covered by *Rolling Stone* magazine under the headline "Newport Pop Festival Drags on in Dust and Heat: Dead, Country Joe, Crosby, Pie Fight Weekend's Highlights":

Above and opposite: Vintage advertisements for the Newport Pop Festival held in 1968. *Author's collection.*

An estimated 140,000 attended the first and probably the last Newport Pop Festival in California's Orange County Aug. 3–4, viewing, among others, Tiny Tim, Jefferson Airplane, Country Joe and the Fish, Grateful Dead, Chambers Brothers, Charles Lloyd, James Cotton Blues Band, Quicksilver Messenger Service, and the Byrds.

The festival was regarded musically successful but on other fronts rather less than pleasing. The performers appeared on a raised stage under a striped canopy, but the young crowds were left sitting or standing in a huge, flat, dusty-dry open field under a broiling sun. Refreshment and rest room facilities were less than adequate and the sound system was not powerful enough to carry the sound to everyone present.

The highlight of the pop fest on the first day (Saturday) seemed to come when Country Joe closed the bill. The hour was late and Orange County officials were threatening to shut off the electricity when the band went on, finally relenting to give the band time for two songs. As they began their first, "1, 2, 3, 4, What Are We Fighting For," the approximately 40,000 young people still on hand rose as if one, cheering, hands held aloft in the "peace sign." During the second number, a long blues, even the cops on stage were grinning and adlibbing a moderate version of the boogaloo.

The second day's climax came when David Crosby started a planned pie fight with Jefferson Airplane. In all, 250 cream pies flew back and forth…and the thousands of people present stormed the stage to join in.

The musical line-up was an impressive one. Besides those already mentioned, bands appearing were Alice Cooper, Steppenwolf, Sonny and Cher, Canned Heat, Electric Flag, Butterfield Blues Band, Eric Burdon and the Animals, Blue Cheer, Iron Butterfly, Illinois Speed Press and Things to Come.

But admission to the festival was $5.50 per day—to sit in heat and dust. Most considered it another in the series of pop music shucks.

Three days after the event, the Costa Mesa City Council decided that there would not be a Newport Pop Festival encore. "To say that we would not like it back here would be the understatement of the year," Costa Mesa mayor Alvin Pinkley was quoted as saying.

In 1968, there was another interesting little musical moment that occurred in Orange County. At a small club called the Cave located near the corner of Beach Boulevard and Adams Avenue in Huntington Beach, just a few blocks from the ocean, the band Them, featuring Van Morrison, performed for one night. Opening the show was ? and the Mysterians, who had just had

Meatloaf's first band, Meatloaf Soul, is pictured on the pier in Huntington Beach in 1968. *Author's collection.*

a hit with the song "96 Tears." And the first band to take the stage was a group called Meatloaf Soul, whose lead singer, Marvin Lee Aday, also went by the name "Meatloaf."

"I remember that gig really well," he recalled. "We went and took a picture on Huntington Beach. Which became like our very first band photo. But what really stands out to me is that was pretty much the first time I ever get up on the stage and sang professionally with a band. So in that sense my musical career as a rock 'n' roll singer was born in Huntington Beach."

Another Orange County venue that served as a magnet for major rock 'n' roll acts was the Anaheim Convention Center Arena, which opened in the summer of 1967 just across the street from Disneyland at 800 West Katella Boulevard. The distinctive Googie-style building held 7,500 people and kicked off its opening night with a performance by

The Doors performed at the Anaheim Convention Center Arena in 1967. *Author's collection.*

The Anaheim Convention Center Arena. *Author's collection.*

the Doors on July 15, 1967. Also on the bill were Jefferson Airplane and Merry Go Round. Not too big and not too small, the arena provided the perfect intimacy for a diverse host of bands over the years. One night you might have Hot Tuna playing with John Mayall. Another might feature a show with Cream and Spirit. Over the years, the arena was used for many different events, from sports to conventions, but one of its primary functions was as a musical venue.

Looking over old concert posters and ads from the Anaheim Convention Center, you get the sense that this building gave Orange County an all-new acceptability in terms of where to play when visiting Southern California. The list of performers is simply jaw dropping.

The Who performed there in September 1967, as did Herman's Hermits. *Donovan in Concert*, the sixth album from the famed British singer-songwriter Donovan (and his very first live album) was recorded at the convention center in September 1967.

And from there, the bands just kept coming.

In January 1968, the Bee Gees performed at the convention center, followed by the Jimi Hendrix Experience, Cream, Janis Joplin, Blue Cheer, Frank Zappa, Creedence Clearwater Revival and Fats Domino.

Within just a year of being open, the Anaheim Convention Center had established itself as a premier concert destination, and all of a sudden, Orange County was part of the main rock 'n' roll circuit.

One of the more notable shows took place on August 9, 1969 (the week before Woodstock would happen back East). Opening the show was a British band called Jethro Tull, and the headliner that evening, on its third tour of the United States, was Led Zeppelin.

Interestingly, Zeppelin had already played Orange County earlier in the year during its spring tour. That show had taken place on May 1, 1969, in Crawford Hall at UC Irvine. It was during this tour that the band took out time at a variety of recording studios around the country to lay down tracks for its forthcoming album, *Led Zeppelin II*. Lee Michaels opened the show at the college, which had been deeply oversold by the school. A second show had actually been scheduled but was not performed. By the time the band came back to Orange County for the August 9 show, it was reportedly earning $30,000 per show. The set list that evening included, "I Can't Quit You Baby," "Dazed and Confused," "You Shook Me" and "Communication Breakdown."

Even more big-name bands came to Anaheim in 1970 to play the convention center arena. A February 7 show featured Jefferson Airplane,

Jethro Tull returned in October to play as a headliner and Grand Funk Railroad arrived in November.

On December 4, 1970, Elton John, on his very first U.S. tour, paid a visit. He had arrived in America that past August and played a string of now legendary shows at the Troubadour club in Los Angeles. He played shows throughout the fall and then wrapped up with the show in Anaheim and then one more in San Bernardino at the Swing Auditorium.

John would return to the Anaheim Convention Center in May 1971. With no other small-sized arena in the area, the venue kept booking interesting popular shows throughout the next several years. In 1973, Crosby, Nash and Young play there, along with Steely Dan, Rod Stewart and the Faces, Emerson Lake and Palmer, the Beach Boys and Elvis Presley (the first of two appearances he would make there).

Presley performed for two nights, April 23 to the 24. Part of a review in the *Anaheim Bulletin* read:

Elvis Presley once more affirmed his role as the "King of Rock 'n' Roll" to overflow crowds at the Anaheim Convention Center. Reminiscent of his recent TV special, Elvis illuminated the stage in a beaded, white pants suit as he strutted out to the pulsating rhythm of "2001"—an appropriate introduction for the man whose genesis was "Hound Dog" and who has left an indelible impression on the evolution of Rock And Roll.

Twenty years and millions of sold records later, only some of the pelvis in Elvis seems to be gone. He had immediate control over his audience from the first song—"C.C. Rider"—until his finale of "Blue Hawaii." His delivery was both melodic and mellow. Ardent fans may have been surprised by his subdued Rhythm and Blues rendition of Hound Dog and later, James Taylor's Steamroller. His showmanship was apparent throughout the night last week as he appealed, with almost sarcastic flare, to all areas of the audience amidst the strobe-like effect of flash bulbs.

Elvis also got a little help from his friends. Included in the production was an exceptionally fine brass orchestra directed by Joe Guercio, his own backup band led by James Burton, the "J.D. Sumner and The Stamps" quartet and soprano Kathy Westmoreland. Miss Westmoreland's obligato was a unique contribution to Elvis' performance of "How Great Thou Art," one of two gospel numbers he included.

The Sweet Inspirations, a soulful female trio, harmonized with Elvis throughout the evening as did the quartet, of whom it was Ray Strampy who had an unbelievable bass voice. The Sweet Inspirations were also one of the lead acts, and were successful in getting the audience warmed up with their rendition of Aretha Franklin's Greatest Hits. Aretha Franklin is one of the many great singers with whom they have appeared."

Actually, in addition to performing in Anaheim in 1973 and '76, Presley has another interesting bit of history in Orange County.

The story begins in the late 1960s, when a Hawaiian-born martial arts instructor named Mike Stone met Elvis and his wife, Priscilla, at a karate competition. Stone, who would eventually relocate to Huntington Beach, ran into the couple again in 1972 at one of Elvis's Las Vegas performances. Soon, at the suggestion of Elvis, Priscilla began learning martial arts under Stone's tutelage. By this time, Stone had opened a school in Westminster, which Presley would drive to from her Los Angeles home. Eventually, she gave up commuting and began training with Chuck Norris, who ran a program closer to her home.

But she also began a romantic relationship with Stone.

This love affair would eventually be the undoing of her marriage with Elvis. In 1975, the couple split and Priscilla had one of her horses, Domino (a gift from Elvis), shipped from Graceland to Huntington Beach, where it lived at the Reynolds Boarding Stables, owned and operated by Betty and Rex Reynolds.

Their son, Cody Reynolds, told me from San Francisco, where he now lives, that he had fond memories of both Priscilla and her young daughter, Lisa Marie.

"It was a beautiful time in Huntington Beach," he shared. "Very laid-back and peaceful. We always enjoyed when Priscilla would come down to ride her horse. She was very beautiful, and we enjoyed her company. Nobody ever called her Priscilla though. To everyone at the stables she was known as 'Beau.'" (Perhaps derived from her maiden name, Beaulieu.)

"Lisa Marie was pretty young then and rather than ride horses, she would spend time in the playground that we had at the stables." (Located today on Goldenwest near Central Library.)

OK, so we have established that Priscilla Presley, her daughter with Elvis and a gift horse from Elvis used to spend some time in Huntington Beach.

But what about the King himself?

In the early 1970s, Presley had also started taking martial arts lessons from Mike Stone (who had become a tenth-degree black belt). However, Elvis was too big a celebrity to take classes at Stone's Westminster studio. Rather, Presley would visit the trainer at his home, located in a housing tract on Edwards Avenue between Warner and Heil Avenues.

Jay Meyers, who lived just around the corner from Stone in the early 1970s, explained to me how he would often see Elvis in the neighborhood: "I was in my early teens and as kids we would see the limo pull into the tract. We'd be riding our bikes and recognized the limo after a few times, and he would roll down the window and wave to us. It made us feel on top of the world that Elvis waved at us."

And while the Anaheim Convention Center Arena saw plenty of legendary music through the late '60s and early 70s, the smaller Melodyland was still going strong, as well.

Throughout the late 1960s, many popular musical artists—including Jackie Wilson, the Righteous Brothers, Linda Ronstadt, Jose Feliciano, the Association, the Strawberry Alarm Clock and Jefferson Airplane—all performed at Melodyland. In 1969, Melodyland closed down and was taken over by the Christian Center, Church of Anaheim. Gone were the days of the Grateful Dead playing there; now the building played host to noted speakers from the charismatic Pentecostal movement. It was torn down in 2003.

The stadium rock era arrived in Orange County on June 14, 1970, when the Who brought its *Tommy* tour to town. The show, which also featured John Sebastian, Leon Russell and Blues Image, is still fondly recalled by fans who were in attendance.

And it ushered in a new era in Orange County concert experience. Within the next several years, huge crowds would flock to the baseball stadium to see myriad big-name acts, including Chicago, who played the venue in May 1975; Fleetwood Mac, who visited in August 1975; and the Eagles, who performed the month after that.

The Who would return to Anaheim Stadium in 1976, followed shortly after by the Beach Boys, America, Yes, Peter Frampton and Aerosmith. On August 20, 1976, Kiss played one of the most memorable shows in its history at the ballpark.

As Kiss guitarist/vocalist Paul Stanley shared:

Playing right over there was a milestone for us. We were four guys from New York City who had nothing—we didn't have a pot to piss in. But we had a dream. And when you use a dream as a template for what you want, then your dream becomes a map. And our map led us there before any other stadium. And so we feel a connection to this area. This is hallowed ground for us. In a sense, there are different places in the country that we mark, but this one was a turning point for us.

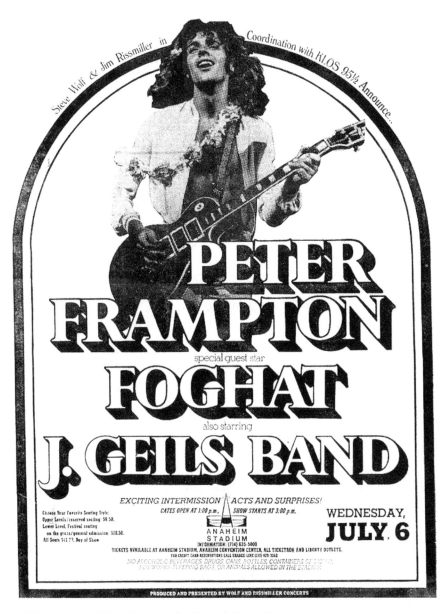

A 1970s concert ad from Anaheim Stadium. *Author's collection.*

Throughout the '70s and for the next several decades after, Anaheim Stadium would continue to host some of the largest and most lavish productions in rock history, including Pink Floyd's *Animals* tour in 1977.

The album art for a bootleg recording of Kiss's legendary show at Anaheim Stadium in 1976. *Author's collection.*

Right: An early
promotional shot of
the Everly Brothers.
Author's collection.

Opposite, bottom:
The Good Time
Theater at Knott's
Berry Farm is where
the Everly Brothers
broke up in 1973.
Author's collection.

But there was still an active club scene in Orange County in addition to all the pomp and big production happening at Anaheim Stadium and at the nearby convention center.

Somewhat controversially, the famed Everly Brothers, on July 14, 1973, at Knott's Berry Farms' John Wayne Theater (later to be called the Good Time Theater), nearly came to a permanent halt. They'd been bickering for years, but it all came to a head midway through the second of three scheduled shows. The band's manager came on the stage and halted the show. He explained to the audience that he was upset with Don Everly's sloppy performance. Phil Everly in turn smashed his guitar on stage and then abruptly left. Don Everly announced to the stunned crowd that the Everly Brothers had split. Quoting Don, "The Everly Brothers died ten years ago."

Not until September 23, 1983, did the Everly Brothers make peace with one another and reunite.

But the Good Time Theater at Knott's would continue to book big-name pop acts throughout the 1970s and '80s. Like Disneyland, as a theme park, Knott's had also discovered the many benefits of creating an in-park venue for added entertainment value.

The Golden Bear in Huntington Beach continued to thrive. In 1974, it was purchased by the brothers Rick and Chuck Babiracki, along with Rick's wife, Carole. They continued building the legacy of the Bear by booking many of the more relevant and meaningful touring bands of the mid-1970s.

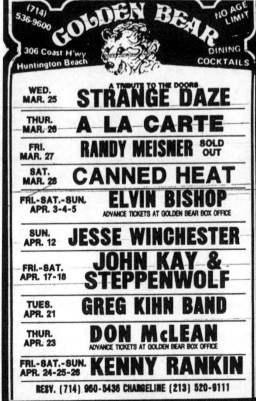

Above: The outdoor stage at Knott's Berry Farm where teen pop sensations Menudo were performing in the 1980s. *Author's collection.*

Left: A vintage ad from the Golden Bear in Huntington Beach illustrates just how diverse its lineups could be during any given week. *Author's collection.*

Jerry Garcia, Muddy Waters, Patti Smith, the Ramones, Arlo Guthrie and many others flocked to the intimate ocean-side club located right by the pier in Huntington Beach.

Today, former owner Carole Babiracki has many fond memories. "The night singer Tom Waits crashed on the floor among beer cases and pulled a Big Mac from his pocket before uttering, 'You never know when you'll get hungry.' Or when actor Christopher Reeve came down to visit his pal Robin Williams, who was performing standup. How about reggae singer Peter Tosh's request for five fresh red snappers so his chef could make fish-head stew?"

I interviewed Peter Gabriel recently and asked him if it was true if he, after playing the Bear on his first solo tour in the late 1970s, went for an evening ocean dip after his show. I'd heard the rumors over the years. "Oh, absolutely," Gabriel chuckled wistfully in his soft-spoken British accent. "A lovely venue in a lovely town. Me and the whole band actually, just [went] out the back door and down to the beach, right after we played. A magnificent evening. I'll never forget it. What a perfect location for a club that was."

Gabriel played another memorable show in Orange County on June 17, 1980, at a small venue called the Santa Ana Club House, which was located at 2720 North Main Street in Santa Ana. The club had been open for about ten years at that point and would book bands that had also played the Golden Bear and the Marina Palace. Gabriel, though, had decided to squeeze in a small club show during a tour in which he was playing larger theaters, so the demand for tickets was quite high.

Sponsored by the radio station KROQ, the "secret" Peter Gabriel show was heavily promoted, and as a result, there were about 1,000 fans packed into a space that could only hold about 250. Gabriel and his band were over an hour late for the show, and things were tense in the claustrophobic space. A bootleg recording of the show exists and it's clear from Gabriel's onstage patter that there were all kinds of issues inside the club. Gabriel said, "I've just been told that we have somewhat of a serious problem. We have exceeded the fire limit here, I'll be back." And then soon after he continued, "I've been really trying hard to persuade them to let us finish off, but there's absolutely no way, hold on, hold on the power will be pulled!"

In the late '70s, an unknown muralist named Wyland painted a mural on the outside of the Golden Bear. He explained, "I was sitting in the Golden Bear one night watching B.B. King play. And I was sitting there doing a sketch. The owner of the club, Rick Babiracki, came over and asked what I was doing. I told him that I was a muralist and I was sketching some of the artists who have played the club. He asked when I could start painting on the side of the building, and I said, 'Tomorrow.'" And so he did. This was long before Wyland became famous for painting what he calls the Whaling Walls.

Over at Disneyland, they were still bringing in the occasional musical act to perform on what was called the Tomorrowland stage (located where the Space Mountain roller coaster is today). Of all the shows that took place there in the '70s, arguably the most important one was on July 12, 1971. Linda Ronstadt needed a backup band for a one-off gig at the theme park. The guy she was dating at the time, singer-songwriter J.D. Souther, was friendly with a group of guys he knew from hanging out and playing at the Troubadour club in Los Angeles. Their names were Don Henley, Glenn Frey, Randy Meister and Bernie Leadon. Although a couple of the guys had backed Ronstadt before, this was the first time that the four of them had ever played together, thus marking the birth night of a band that

would go on to become the Eagles.

For all the major-name bands that would start visiting Orange County in the 1970s, it wasn't as if there was no local scene or local bands. One group in particular managed to capture the heart and soul of the county like no other band of the early '70s.

Formed in 1970 in Laguna Beach, the band

The exterior of the Golden Bear in Huntington Beach featured the signature of famed marine life artist Wyland, who painted this while still relatively unknown. *Author's collection.*

64

The Tomorrowland stage at Disneyland is where the Eagles were born. *Author's collection.*

known as Honk still lives on to this day as one of the most sentimental favorites of the area. Eclectic, diverse and even somewhat experimental, its loose and airy beach vibe made it popular in clubs from the outset.

But as the band's drummer, Tris Imboden, described, the band's history and trajectory took a strange course that its members never saw coming:

> *I grew up in Sunset Beach, and then we moved over to Huntington Harbor. So I'm Orange County through and through. I grew up practicing with bands in our garage. I grew up playing in surf bands like a lot of other kids and then moved to Newport Beach, where I continued playing in bands.*
>
> *There was a band called New Life, and I was just a kid; still they asked me to join, which was really exciting. They were the band that went on to became Honk. We started playing in clubs in Laguna Beach at a place called the Orphanage. We played covers mostly, but we'd sneak in some originals we were working on. We really had designs of being an all-original band. The unique thing about Honk was they*

already had a record deal without even being an official band. See, New Life had been signed to a label already and so it just sort of carried over with Honk.

We were approached by the makers of the surf films, the great directors Greg McGillivray and Jim Freeman. Jim has since passed away. But those two brilliant guys said that he knew a couple of us in the band were surfers, and we had become so popular as a band in Orange County that even though we were anything but a surf band, they wanted us to do music for this film they were making called Five Summer Stories. *It was only described to us, and so we had to imagine what we were writing to. It really was like Zen archery, but we did it—we just wrote the music for this film. And when we saw what they had put together at the Santa Monica Civic Auditorium, it was incredible. And they even had us play a special concert before the screening. And it just fit so perfectly. So unwittingly we became modern-day surf band heroes. We had a number-one record in Hawaii, an instrumental called* Pipeline Sequence, *and our popularity went through the roof. The film helped spread our name around and we had mixed emotions about it because we were not a surf band. We were all over the map—a really, an eclectic bunch of musicians. Jazz to folk to R&B. And our originals reflected that.*

In our ultimate heyday, we sold out a full week at the Troubadour, and that was really our zenith. We opened for everybody from Loggins and Messina to the Beach Boys. And we finally signed with Epic Records.

I think the reason we did so well in Orange County is that we just represented the mood of the time. Laguna Beach was the perfect launching point for us because it was very laid-back and very artsy and creative. We were hippies of that sort, and so we just fit in perfectly there. But we also did really well in Huntington Beach whenever we played the Golden Bear, which was a lot. There were some really good bands around the area at that time, but everybody seemed to like and appreciate the fact that we were trying to do something original. That we were not just happy being a cover band. With Five Summer Stories, *we really kind of became solidified as his hometown heroes.*

Imboden went on to have a successful and varied career as drummer for the Kenny Loggins band, with whom he played on the number-one soundtracks for the prominent 1980s films *Caddyshack* and *Footloose*. Since 1990, he's been the full-time drummer with the band Chicago. But for all he has done, he can never get Honk out of his system.

THE LATE 1960s–MID-1970s

Hometown heroes Honk as they looked in the mid-1970s. *Author's collection.*

"We still get together when we can to have some fun and remember the good times. No matter where I go or what I do, it's impossible for me not to recall fondly the Orange County music scene of the 1970s. It was vital, it was important and it was a lot of fun for many of us, whether we were busy playing in a band or just hanging out at clubs [or] at the Golden Bear watching our musical heroes."

From the music industry standpoint, another big event that took place in 1977 was the arrival of the NAMM show to Anaheim California. One of the two largest music product tradeshows in the world, NAMM (which stands for the National Association of Music Merchants) has been held in Anaheim each year since then. The trade-only business show, which caters to domestic and international dealers and distributors, also boasts one of the biggest gatherings of the biggest names in music each January in Anaheim, where musicians both perform and explore the hundreds of product exhibits that are the mainstay of the show. As a result, whenever a big name is in town, there are many concerts and other musical events that take place around the county, which are all connected to the NAMM show.

While the show is not open to the public, it still remains one of the hottest tickets with many people scrambling to find a connection through either a dealer or artist that might be able to gain them access.

67

Throughout the show, there are many concerts, booth appearances and intimate performances held throughout the Anaheim Convention Center. Interestingly, the Anaheim Convention Center Arena, which has hosted so many legendary concerts over the years, is typically taken over by distributors for the event. One wonders if all the dealers and salesmen in that portion of the event are aware of the fact that they are standing where legends such as Led Zeppelin, Elvis Presley, David Bowie, Cream, Elton John and many others performed memorable shows over the years?

Something else happened in 1977. A little band from Pasadena named Van Halen came down to play the old Retail Clerks Auditorium in Buena Park on October 8. In a few months, the band would head out on its first ever national tour, with Journey and Montrose, just after releasing its debut album in February 1978. It wasn't the first time the band had played Orange County, though. In January 1977, Van Halen had performed at the Golden Bear. The band appeared with a band called Yesterday & Today (soon to become simply Y&T), and the guys in Van Halen told the club owner, "Take our picture; we will be famous some day." So she did.

Chapter 3

THE LATE 1970s–EARLY 1980s

When the Rolling Stones first came to Orange County in 1978, near the end of their *Some Girls* tour to play back-to-back shows at Anaheim Stadium on July 23 and 24, it marked a triumphant moment for the band. Unlike the band's previous American tour in 1975, this show was not based on any sort of major production like the elaborate lotus petal stage it had trucked around the world. For the Stones, it'd all be about stripping down. The stage show was sparse and minimal to match the raw and passionate fire of the album they were promoting this time, *Some Girls*. The Stones would return to that ballpark a number of times over the years, and many who were there in 1978 recall with glee the energy and intensity of the show. But while the Stones had started to embrace the punk ethos ignited a couple years before by bands like the Ramones and the Sex Pistols, in Orange County there were a number of bands that were channeling the same kind of anger, rebellion and do-it-yourself approach.

In the city of Fullerton, a teenager named Mike Ness—inspired by the Sex Pistols and the same band that was packing Anaheim Stadium that summer, the Rolling Stones—formed a band called Social Distortion, along with drummer Casey Royer and brothers Frank and Rikk Agnew, who played bass and guitar, respectively. Before the band recorded its debut album, the Agnew brothers left Social Distortion to join the Adolescents, another Fullerton punk band that also featured members from Agent Orange.

As the *OC Weekly* described Agent Orange:

[It was] *formed by a cranky, pissed-off 14-year-old named Mike Palm—sounded distinctly Orange County, as opposed to the mostly slash-and-burn approach perpetrated by their peers Social Distortion and the Adolescents. That's because they injected Dick Dale–inspired surf-guitar breaks and more overt melody lines amidst all the usual thrashiness.* In 1981, they released the Living In Darkness *album, which included "Bloodstains"—not just a classic OC punk tune, but a classic tune period. The band's largest following, though, came via an army of skateboarders. They were one of the first bands to tap into the then-still-kind-of-underground subculture, putting their music on the soundtracks of various skate videos. After all this time, Palm still hasn't gotten a real job, and still tours as Agent Orange with a revolving lineup of players.*

Back to the Adolescents, though—they became one of the leading-edge bands of the 1980s hard-core punk scene. They juggled members many times over the course of thirty years, but their self-titled 1981 debut remains one of the most seminal albums in hard-core punk history.

Social Distortion finally recorded its debut album, *Mommy's Little Monster*, in 1983. The band would not record a follow-up for four years, during which time Ness descended into heroin addiction. Regardless, it was an integral part of what became one of the most important punk movements in the world despite being scattered throughout the unlikely and mostly lily-white bedroom communities of Orange County.

A flyer for a show held at New Klub on the Block Costa Mesa. *Courtesy of Ernie Grimm.*

The Late 1970s–Early 1980s

Also in 1978, one of Huntington Beach's first, if not *the* punk band from Surf City also formed. It was called the Crowd and was put together by brothers Jim and Jay Decker, along with guitarist Jim Kaa and, later, drummer Dennis Walsh. Together for just a couple years, and despite its growing popularity throughout Orange County, in 1982 the band broke up. But in 1987, it found its way back again and continues to make music today with a variety of solo projects and the occasional crowd project as well. The Crowd may have only been together for a brief time at the inception of the Orange County punk movement, but the band was still highly influential. Some punk aficionados think that frontman Jim Decker actually invented slam dancing.

Another band generally credited with igniting a chunk of the West Coast hard-core punk movement also came from Fullerton. The Middle Class consisted of brothers Jeff Atta on vocals, Mike Atta on guitar and Bruce Atta on drums with Mike Patton on bass. Though they never achieved the success or notoriety of Social Distortion, in a number of other homegrown Orange County punk bands, they remain deeply respected and influential for those who either saw them play or heard one of their few releases.

As Matt Coker wrote in the *Orange County Weekly* in 2002:

> *"Many hold the Middle Class up as probably the first American hardcore band, which basically meant playing faster downbeat tempos than the first wave of 'Hollywood' proto-hardcore bands like the Germs and the Bags," says Brendan Mullen, founder of the Masque, the Hollywood underground club/rehearsal space considered to be the birthplace of the Los Angeles and Orange County punk scenes…The Atta boys are more surprised than anyone that the Middle Class, which disbanded in 1982, is credited with launching a form of music that was quickly picked up by TSOL and the Circle Jerks, music that soldiers on with Narcoleptic Youth and Litmus Green. Well, they're more surprised than anyone outside of their band mates, brother Bruce Atta (drums) and Mike Patton (bass).*
>
> *"Twenty years later, you can look at it and say hardcore is where we fit," Mike Atta says, "but we never felt we were trying to start anything."*

The Vandals formed in Huntington Beach in 1980. Guitarist Jan Nils Ackermann, singer Steven Jensen, bassist Steve Pfauter and drummer Joe Esclante, in almost no time at all, built a solid reputation both in Orange County and up in Los Angeles, along with other relevant punk bands of the time, including Bad Religion, Black Flag, T.S.O.L. (True Sounds of Liberty), X, the Germs, Suicidal Tendencies and, of course, Social Distortion.

In 1984, the Vandals would appear in the film *Suburbia*, directed by Penelope Spheeris who had already directed the well-known punk documentary *The Decline of Western Civilization*. Perhaps infamously, they also would play a benefit concert that year in Orange County for the Cypress College Young Republicans, being joined with other punk stalwarts the Circle Jerks and the Dickies, among others. The performance drew heavy criticism from the anarchy-driven punk community.

T.S.O.L. also came together in Huntington Beach in 1978. Originally composed of singer Jack Grisham, guitarist Ron Emery, bassist Mike Roche and drummer Todd Barnes, the band's first EP was released in 1981, followed up soon after by a full-length album entitled *Dance with Me*. Its goth and hard-core stylings immediately made an impact. Throughout the '80s, T.S.O.L. would morph into a more glam metal band, and all original band members would eventually be replaced. However, in 1991, the original members returned, and they started making music again. The last studio album, *Life, Liberty and the Pursuit of Free Downloads* was released in 2009.

Another influential punk band that grew out of the sand and surf in Huntington Beach was China White. Named for the heroin that killed Germs lead singer Darby Crash and inspired by the punk anthem "Chinese Rocks," the band originally included vocalist Scott Sisunik, guitarists Frank Ruffino and Marc Martin, bassist James Rodriguez and drummer Richard Katchadoorian (later replaced by Vince Mesa).

An 1985 ad for a China White show in Garden Grove. *Courtesy of Ernie Grimm.*

After hammering it out on both the Orange County and Los Angeles club circuits, in 1981 China White signed to Frontier Records. Its first EP, entitled *Danger Zone*, was infamous for its front cover depicting a murder scene. The band would split up several years later, but the band has

An ad for a show held at the Cuckoo's Nest in Costa Mesa. *Courtesy of Ernie Grimm.*

regrouped occasionally over the years with a variety of new members.

Along with Social Distortion and T.S.O.L., China White's legacy remains burned in the punk rock history of Orange County. In 2013, guitarist Frank Ruffino became ill and was in need of a new liver. Bands, including Bad Religion, Black Flag, the Adolescents and many more, donated items for an auction to raise funds for the ailing punk legend. Benefit concerts were also held, but sadly, Ruffino passed away on June 4, 2013.

The fertile punk rock scene in Orange County meant, of course, that there would need to be venues to accommodate the intense and often physical shows where slam dancing and early forms of mosh pits were evolving. The Golden Bear was far too tame for many of these bands, and so other venues began to almost spontaneously pop up around the county.

The Cuckoo's Nest, which was open at 1714 Placentia Avenue in Costa Mesa from 1978 to 1981, became one of the first true punk rock ground zeros in Orange County. But it was never without controversy. Hosting such local favorites as Social Distortion, Agent Orange and others, owner Jerry Roach constantly had his hands full, in large part due to the fact that located right next door to his punk club was a restaurant called Zubies, which was typically populated by a country music–loving crowd. Fights between the two factions became legendary but eventually city officials revoked Roach's entertainment permits and put his club out of business—but not before its legendary status was etched into the minds of punk fans who traveled far and wide to visit the vaunted venue.

The 1981 film on the club, called *Urban Struggle*, detailed not just how local punks attending the club were constantly being harassed by the

This ad for legendary punk band Black Flag is from when it played the Cuckoo's Nest in Costa Mesa. *Courtesy of Ernie Grimm.*

law but also how Roach felt that authorities were actually trying to stamp out something they considered to be simply a violent fad.

The Cuckoo's Nest is famed for being the first place to ever have a "slam pit." But more important are the bands that it hosted, which went beyond the modern-day punk heroes like Circle Jerks, Bad Brains, Dead Kennedys and the Dickies. The club also saw appearances from a wide range of artists who no doubt inspired many of the young punks who were forming bands in the late '70s and early '80s. Velvet Underground legend John Cale, the Damned, the Ramones, XTC, Squeeze, Iggy Pop and the Cramps all spent time at the Cuckoo's Nest.

It may not have been there long, but in many ways, the Cuckoo's Nest was to Orange County what CBGB was to New York City, a musical underground birthplace that caused significant culture shifts.

In 1982, the club reopened under new name, the Concert Factory. There was a new owner and an entirely new slate of bands, ranging from heavy metal to new wave, that came into play. But it didn't last long. Eventually, the building became part of the Zubies complex before being demolished altogether in the late 1990s.

But the place lives on in the music. That's because the club was immortalized in a song called "Pat Brown" by the Vandals—a true story about a punk fan who allegedly tried to run over two cops outside the Cuckoo's Nest, thus prompting one of them to fire shots into his fleeing car.

Guitar Legend Dick Dale first opened a nightclub in Riverside in 1968, and in the early 1970s, he purchased a beer bar called the Playgirl Club in Garden Grove. He renamed it the Rendezvous in homage to the ballroom in Balboa where he became famous and, over time, expanded it into an eighteen-thousand-square-foot music megaplex. He appeared there often, booked big touring bands and, eventually, opened Rendezvous II in Huntington Beach.

It might be worth noting here that while it may seem like all the rock 'n' roll history in Orange County was testosterone fueled, if we backtrack a few years to the mid-1970s, something happened before the punk movement that was certainly influential.

As Suzanne Rush noted in *Record Collector* magazine in 2013:

An ad for the legendary punk club the Cuckoo's Nest in Costa Mesa. *Courtesy of Ernie Grimm.*

The band that spawned one of rock's most durable female icons was born in a suburban rec room in greater Los Angeles. Suzi Quatro–wannabe, Joan Larkin, had to take four buses from the San Fernando Valley to meet up with drummer Sandy Pesavento at her Brady Bunch–like homestead in Huntington Beach. But, the moment the two 16-year-olds began to jam on "All Shook Up," they knew they'd finally found rock 'n' roll compatriots. This guitar-drum duo, who rechristened themselves Joan Jett and Sandy West, would form the nucleus of The Runaways, the first all-girl rock band to get a record contract. The rest of the lineup would variously include: Micki Steele, Lita Ford, Cherie Currie and an ever-changing roster of bass players.

Standing outside West's home today in Huntington Beach, it's hard to believe that the Runaways were essentially born in the small suburban garage. Yet they were. And while West never achieved the superstardom of her cohort Joan Larkin, her legacy literally remains carved into Orange County.

The Runaways. *Author's collection.*

Sadly, West passed away from cancer in 2006 at the age of just forty-seven. But in 2013, in the southern Orange County city of Dana Point, a special memorial was dedicated to her. Her band mate Cherie Currie, who is now a well-known wood sculptor, created a sculpture in her honor. It depicts a mermaid playing electric guitar and was commissioned by Kenny's Music Store in Dana Point as a tribute to West. On the memorial pedestal that supports the sculpture, Currie inlaid a pair of West's drumsticks. The store where the memorial is located is at 24731 LaPlaza in Dana Point.

While punk rock may have been flourishing in Orange County in the early 1980s, it didn't preclude the introduction of larger venues to accommodate bigger-name acts as the county's population continued to grow. By this time, the Anaheim Convention Center Arena was not booking nearly as many shows as it once had, and it was too small to accommodate many of the larger commercial acts that were touring nationally. Fortunately, in 1980, the Irvine Meadows Amphitheater was built by the Irvine Company. The facility opened in 1981 and automatically became a magnet for arena touring acts. The very first year it opened, the amphitheater hosted Tom Petty and the Heartbreakers, Dan Fogelberg and Ozzy Osbourne. In fact, a live concert performance by Osborne recorded on June 12, 1982, entitled *Speak of the Devil*, was released in 2012.

The Grateful Dead performed fifteen times at the amphitheater between 1983 and 1989, and another musical legacy was established there by the band Oingo Boingo, which played its annual Halloween concerts there from 1986 through 1991 and one final time in 1993 before moving the shows to the Universal Amphitheater in Los Angeles.

Michael Jackson came through in November 1988 on his *Bad* tour, and given the open space around the amphitheater, it has been the site of many festivals, including Uproar, Gigantour, Lilith Fair and Lollapalooza.

Since its opening, the name has been changed to the Verizon Wireless Amphitheater. As of this writing, the amphitheater's lease expires in 2017, and according to published reports, the Irvine Company has plans to demolish the amphitheater and build apartment buildings on the site.

In Costa Mesa California, at the Orange County Fairgrounds where the aforementioned Pop Festival was held in 1968, the Pacific Amphitheater was opened in 1983. With a capacity of 18,500, it also saw its share of big-name shows early on. Most notable perhaps is the fact that Marvin Gaye performed his last ever concert at this venue on August 14, 1983. It was during the ill-fated *Sexual Healing* tour, which often saw Gaye's performances affected by his heavy cocaine use. At the end of the show, the Motown legend went to live at his parents' house in Los Angeles, and almost a year later to the day, on April 1, 1984, Gaye died after being shot by his father.

For all of the thousands who flocked to the two sparkling new amphitheaters in Orange County in the

melvins

w/

DIRT CLOD FIGHT

THE**HAGS**   FU MANCHU

SAT. APR 18

BOOKING INFO-CRAIG AT 714-650-1141
CLUB INFO-650-1840

NEW KLUB ON THE BLOCK
1700 Placentia Ave, Costa Mesa
Corner of Placentia and 17th.
At The Newport Roadhouse

An ad for the New Klub on the Block located in Costa Mesa. *Courtesy of Ernie Grimm.*

LIVE AT CLUB CANNIBAL
SATURDAY   THE
OCT. 21   VANDALS

SAMSONS
ARMY
AND
SPECIAL
GUEST'S

LOCATED AT MEADOWLARK COUNTRY CL
16782 GRAHAM
HUNTINGTON BEACH
FOR INFO. CALL (7H) 964-9413

DRINK SPECIALS BEFORE 11:0
21 WITH ID
DOORS OPEN AT 9:30

AT THE CORNER OF WARNER AND GRAHAM

A flyer for a show the Vandals did at Meadowlark Country Club in Huntington Beach. *Courtesy of Ernie Grimm.*

early '80s, arguably just as many were seeking out the many places were hard-core punk music was thriving. All one has to do is thumb through many old flyers and homemade handouts that were slapped up against light posts over the years to get a sense of just how active the scene was.

Looking over the collection of former punk rock promoter and current memorabilia collector Ernie Grimm, one is transported back in time. Many colorful flyers promote shows at the Meadowlark Country Club in Huntington Beach featuring Gypsy Trash, Hellbent, the Vandals, Samson's Army and others.

At the Old World faux-German center in Huntington Beach, flyers advertise shows by the Crowd, Simple Tones, Rik L Rik and dozens of others.

At a club called Radio City, located on the corner of Knott and Ball Roads in Anaheim, Cathedral of Tears, featuring members of T.S.O.L. and Middle Class, was playing with Psycho Bud. There were two other clubs located in the strip mall where Radio City was, the Woodstock and Cartoons & Capers.

This flyer was for a show held at the Newport Roadhouse in Costa Mesa featuring Dee Dee Ramone. *Courtesy of Ernie Grimm.*

There was Spangler's Café at 3009 Ball Road in Anaheim, plus an untold number of hardscrabble venues that were simply old VFW halls, warehouses and other makeshift, one-step-ahead-of-the-law performance spaces.

And coming of age within the scene were soon-to-be rock stars. Original Metallica member and founder of Megadeth, Dave Mustaine attended Marina High School in Huntington Beach in the late 1970s.

Shirley Orlando was owner of Huntington Music at Goldenwest Street and Warner Avenue, where she worked for twenty-six years. She ran the place, and in addition to its being a music store, the space was also a haven for musicians in the area—a place where late-night jam sessions were a common occurrence.

Left: An ad for a show that took place at Sargenti's, located in Costa Mesa. *Courtesy of Ernie Grimm.*

Below: An ad for a show at Radio City located in Anaheim. *Courtesy of Ernie Grimm.*

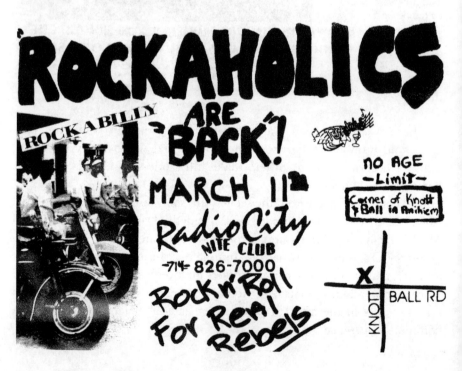

THE LATE 1970S—EARLY 1980S

Heavy metal legend Dave Mustaine attended Marina High School in Huntington Beach. *Courtesy of Charles Epting.*

And yes, Orlando is correct when recounting the intense teenage guitarist who used to shred in her shop. It was Dave Mustaine, founder of the metal band Megadeth.

"We had other big names in that store, too," she told me. "The famous jazz players George Van Epps, Tony Ricci. There were more, too. It was a happening place!"

Scott Weiland, who in the late 1980s would found Stone Temple Pilots with Robert Deleo, attended Edison High School in Huntington Beach in the 1980s.

As vital and formative as the Orange County punk rock movement was, in the mid- to late '80s, it would begin morphing much in the same way that it was in cities like Los Angeles. Hair metal, heavy metal and various other hybrids, many of which owed their energy to punk rock, would soon start to reshape the music scene in Orange County.

On a sad note, in 1986, Orange County lost the famed Golden Bear in Huntington Beach. The city was going through a major amount of redevelopment and the costs involved in retrofitting the brick building for seismic compliance were simply too high for the owners. The final performance at the Golden Bear was on January 29, 1986, by guitarist Robin Trower.

In the last couple of years of its existence, the Golden Bear started booking metal bands. This ad is from 1984. *Author's collection.*

THE LATE 1970s–EARLY 1980s

To this day, many Orange County locals lament the fact that this legendary music landmark was not preserved. One of those people is Robert Carvounas, who may just be the biggest Golden Bear fan of all. In fact, the Huntington Beach local wrote a book about the famed musical landmark and has collected a huge amount of artifacts—photos, tickets, posters, matchbooks, bricks and other memorabilia. "I think it's the most interesting place in Huntington Beach history," he said.

He wasn't of age in the 1960s, so he couldn't see Janis Joplin or the Byrds perform at the Bear, but he did attend several shows in the '80s before it was demolished.

Portions of the structure were preserved and incorporated into the façade of a new Golden Bear that opened several years later. Unfortunately, that incarnation failed quickly, and the club quickly disappeared in the blur and rebuilding of downtown. As Carvounas and I walked over to the site recently, he pointed out where the entrance would have been—where a hot dog place is today. Around the corner, the ticket booth from the second Golden Bear remains, the last trace of a legend—or is it?

As Carvounas explains, collecting pieces of the Golden Bear is a hobby for more than a few people, as a way of holding on to the memories. A planter outside a downtown home is made of Golden Bear bricks, as is another fan's fireplace. A small piece of the structure rests in a local flower garden, and Carvounas himself has one of the exterior signs. "Lots of people grabbed pieces of the place," he said. "Because of the memories. There's never been another place like it here."

But as fate had it, the very year that the Golden Bear was demolished, another intimate club opened that would help pick up the slack where the Bear left off. Even though it's located in a strip mall as opposed to next to the ocean, the Coach House in San Juan Capistrano was opened in 1986 by Gary Folgner, and right away, it became known for its warm and intimate setting that allowed concertgoers the chance to sit within arm's length of some of the biggest names in music. It took a little while to get started, but within a couple years, the pictures that adorn the walls told the story of what was happening at a little club in south Orange County. Artists as notable as Ray Charles, Mick Taylor, Bonnie Raitt and Miles Davis all played inside the Coach House. So, too, did Johnny Thunders from the New York Dolls, along with an early version of the Red Hot Chili Peppers, Jerry Lee Lewis, Todd Rundgren, Carl Perkins and Johnny Cash.

To this day, the Coach House remains one of the most comfortable and classic places to watch music. But back when it was getting started in the mid-1980s, there were a host of other clubs and musical styles with which to contend.

Chapter 4

THE MID-1980s–EARLY 1990s

The next wave of new clubs and bands in Orange County was about to emerge.

Were it not for a riot at a 1984 Social Distortion show in Irvine, the Offspring might never have happened. The Huntington Beach punk band, including guitarist/singer Bryan "Dexter" Holland and bassist Greg Kriesel, was inspired after that concert. The original members had already begun tinkering in a garage in Cyprus, but it was the Social Distortion show that led them to form a band called Manic Subsidal. Soon, they added vocalist Doug Thompson and drummer Jim Benton. Thompson would eventually leave, Holland would take over vocals and Benton would be replaced by James Lilja on the drums. In 1985, Kein Wasserman came aboard as a second guitarist, and a year later, the group became officially known as the Offspring. It wouldn't sign a record deal for another couple years, and though it took several albums and tours to truly establish itself, by the early 1990s, the Offspring had truly arrived. Its 1994 album, entitled *Smash*, featured a number of hit singles, including "Come Out and Play," "Self Esteem" and "Gotta Get Away." At that time, the release set an all-time record for most albums sold by an indie-label band, clocking in at sixteen million units.

There have been some lineup adjustments over the years, but the Offspring has remained one of the biggest musical success stories to come out of Orange County, and it is a band that was generated by some of Orange County's original punk roots. The band's music has appeared in many films

A promotional shot of the Offspring. *Author's collection.*

and video games. The group has truly found a way to blend commercial viability with an original punk rock sound.

In 1986, the year the Offspring adopted its name, another band influenced by Orange County's punky and eclectic roots was also formed. It started when Eric Stefani and John Spence met at a local Dairy Queen and started kicking the idea around of forming a band.

In an unassuming Anaheim garage, Eric, his sister Gwen, Spence, Jerry McMahon, Gabe Gonzalas, Chris Leal and Alan and Tony Meade began practicing.

Going by the name No Doubt, the fledgling band was all but derailed in December 1987, when Spence, the lead vocalist, killed himself shortly before the band was to play a showcase gig at the Roxy Theater in Los Angeles for a host of record label executives. The band initially decided to quit but, after several weeks, reconsidered its decision. Soon, Eric's sister Gwen was singing lead vocals for the band.

Over the course of the next few years, No Doubt built a loyal and rabid following throughout Southern California. The band's ska-infused music, which also incorporated elements of pop punk, reggae and alternative rock, struck a huge chord with many fans. Wildly enthusiastic, stage-diving fans made many No Doubt shows something of an event, as did Gwen's compelling onstage presence. In 1990, No Doubt signed a record deal with the newly formed label called Interscope Records. Its self-titled debut album came out in 1992 but was lost in the sea of grunge music that by then had started flowing out of Seattle. There were a series of other releases over the course of the next several years, but it wasn't until the 1995 album *Tragic Kingdom* that No Doubt finally scored mainstream commercial success. The singles "Just a Girl," "Spiderwebs" and "Don't Speak" established No Doubt as a major commercial force, and the group was nominated for two Grammy Awards, Best New Artist and Best Rock Album, in 1997. *Tragic Kingdom* went on to become one of the bestselling albums in history, and Gwen Stefani became nothing short of a pop-culture icon.

And it all started in a small garage on Beacon Street in Anaheim.

In a former doctor's office in Huntington Beach, a punk club called Safari Sam's opened in 1984. While it would only be in business for two years, a lot of punk rock history was crammed into the small 1920s building just off Main Street. Opened by Sam Lanni and Gil Fuhrer, Safari Sam's booked a diverse and intense lineup of bands. Squeezing them into a small space resulted in some of the most intimate and memorable punk rock shows in Orange County history. Several years ago, Lanni posted a message online as he was attempting to open a new Safari Sam's in Hollywood. It read in part:

> *Twenty years ago I opened a club in Huntington Beach, CA called Safari Sam's with my partner, Gil Fuhrer. We believed that there was a desire by audiences to have a place where punk rock music could intertwine with theater and poetry readings, and would enjoy challenging juxtapositions of art, music, literature, and culture. And we were right. For 20 months in 1985 and 1986, Safari Sam's was a cultural center that drew people from all parts of Southern California, until the City of HB closed us down for redevelopment. During that time, we had such now famous acts as Sonic Youth and Social Distortion play to the same packed audiences that came out to see Henry Rollins read poetry or a performance of Beckett's* Endgame. *It was magical.*

And magical it was. On October 13, 1985, an ad in the paper for the club read: "Gazebo T-shirt, As Is and the Statics will play today. Pop Art, Nick Pyzow and Jimmy Townes will appear Saturday. Love 'N' Terror and James Addiction will perform Sunday."

There is a typo in the ad of course, as the band they were referring to was actually Jane's Addiction, the soon-to-be wildly popular Los Angeles rock

Above: The house in Anaheim on Beacon Street where the band No Doubt first was formed. *Author's collection.*

Right: A flyer advertising a show at Safari Sam's in Huntington Beach. *Courtesy of Ernie Grimm.*

MATINEE BENEFIT

TO HELP H.R.D. FUND

Featuring:

TENDER FURY

THE FLOORLORDS

& MAGIC FISH

SUNDAY AFTERNOON JUNE 8

Show Starts At 1:00 PM

SAFARI SAM'S

411 Olive
Huntington Beach
536-6025

Tender Fury Date-Line

(213)496-3177

BOOKINGS & Complaints

An ad for a show at
the popular punk
club Safari Sam's in
Huntington Beach.
Courtesy of Ernie Grimm.

band fronted by Perry Farrell and featuring guitarist Dave Navarro. And it was the very first time the band had ever played as Jane's Addiction.

Jane's Addiction would also go on to play at a variety of other Orange County clubs, including Joshua's Parlour in Westminster, that regularly hosted many up-and-coming alternative rock bands. Originally opened by Troy Tabak and Randy Noteboom, Joshua's Parlour would eventually be renamed the Marquee. Today, the original structure still stands at 7000 Garden Grove Boulevard, but it is now a strip club.

At the same time, club owner Jerry Roach of famed punk establishment the Cuckoo's Nest in Costa Mesa was also still busy on the scene. Since opening his very first club, the Bacchus House in Newport Beach in 1970, Roach had seen a lot of things but nothing like the arson fire in 1985 that destroyed his club Radio City in Anaheim. Primarily an outlet for original heavy metal and hard rock, Radio City had been riding the popularity wave of the hair metal movement streaming down from Los Angeles. Roach

THE VOTES HAVE BEEN TALLIED
-1 Best Underground Band
- 1 Best Hard Rock Band
as voted in 1st Annual L.A. Weekly Music Awards
NOW ORANGE COUNTY CAN FIND OUT WHAT L.A. ALREADY KNOWS

proudly presents

JANES ADDICTION
Wednesday, March 25th

with special guest
COLD SEPTEMBER & JESTERS OF DESTINY

Plus LA's -1 Rock D.J. Joseph from the Cathouse
at
JOSHUA'S PARLOUR
7000 Garden Grove Blvd., Westminster
Every Wednesday Night Hollywood's Finest in Orange County

Right: This advertisement is from when Jane's Addiction played at Joshua's Parlour. *Courtesy of Ernie Grimm.*

Below: Today, the metal club Joshua's Parlour is a gentleman's club. *Author's collection.*

always had a knack for keeping up with the times as was evidenced by how he transformed the Cuckoo's Nest from a punk club into a rockabilly hall in the early 1980s when that trend was kicked off. Roach was also instrumental in how local shows were marketed. He was one of the first people to encourage local bands to design and print their own tickets, which would entitle fans to a discount while also giving a club owner a distinct way of gauging how popular a group was. In the mid-1980s, he also purchased a Top 40 club called the French Quarter, which was also located in Anaheim. But it failed to take hold, and he quickly sold it at a loss.

In Huntington Beach, a club called Night Moves opened at 5902 Warner Avenue, which catered primarily to punk and alternative bands. Huntington Beach also featured a small club called Spatz located in the Huntington Harbour Mall, where bands such as the Red Hot Chili Peppers and Jane's Addiction played.

Sprinkled throughout the county were other thriving and throbbing venues like the Galaxy Rolling Rink, Ichabods and the Pub.

But arguably the most important punk venue of the era was a tiny Anaheim house called the Doll Hut. It literally had a forty-nine-person capacity, yet it showcased Orange County's most monumental acts, including the

Today, it is called the House of Brews, but back in the mid-1980s, this was Spatz in Huntington Beach. *Author's collection.*

Right: Metal legends Motorhead played in Anaheim and Billy Party's Roller Fantasy in Fullerton. *Courtesy of Ernie Grimm.*

Bottom: The Doll Hut in Anaheim, as it looks today. *Author's collection.*

Offspring, Social Distortion, the Vandals and many others. The funky little building located in the warehouse district was originally constructed in the early 1900s as a private home. In the mid-'30s it became a truck stop café, and there are also rumors that it was even used as a brothel in the 1950s. It was christened the Doll Hut in 1957 and then became a live music venue. But it wasn't until promoter Linda Jemison purchased it in the late 1980s that it became famous in the same way that CBGB did a New York City or the Whisky a Go Go did in Los Angeles.

Jemison rightfully earned her role as a local hero for developing the club into one of the most uniquely intimate and intense venues that has ever existed in the area. Though it closed its doors in the summer of 2001, it has changed ownership a number of times and, to this day, remains open and thriving. It is perhaps the ultimate punk rock landmark in Orange County.

In the mid- to late 1980s, there were still the occasional shows at Angel Stadium in Anaheim. Madonna brought her *Who's That Girl* tour to the ballpark on July 18, 1987. The next week, on July 26, Bob Dylan and the Grateful Dead rolled in for a show. And David Bowie would perform there in 1983, bringing his *Glass Spider* tour in on August 8, 1987.

And in the midst of all the metal clubs and still thriving punk rock clubs, a more middle-of-the-road theater opened in Anaheim in 1987. It was called the Celebrity Theater; it seated 2,500 people, and within its first year, both Chuck Berry and the Red Hot Chili Peppers performed there. It was a theater-in-the-round experience with a stage that slowly spun, giving the entire audience a chance for a full-frontal view. While more "adult" acts like the Beach Boys, George Carlin and Howie Mandel performed there, many rock 'n' roll acts were booked there as well. Bob Weir from the Grateful Dead performed there, as did Fats Domino, the Ramones, Guns N' Roses, Testament, Todd Rundgren, Paul Stanley, the Monkees and many more.

The Celebrity Theater closed in 1994 and reopened three years later as the Freedman Forum, a performing arts venue. That didn't last long though, and today, the building is called the Heritage Forum, which hosts various church services, dance shows and other public events.

And Irvine Meadows Ampitheatre was also going strong. In the mid- to late 1980s, the impressive amphitheater hosted a dazzling and diverse number of artists, including Elton John, Judas Priest, David Gilmour, Elvis Castillo, the Smiths, Depeche Mode, Iron Maiden, Def Leppard, Bon Jovi and dozens more. They all performed at the site formerly occupied by the Lion Country Safari theme park, nestled into the green hills just off the freeway.

Over the course of a couple decades, Orange County had as wide a range of performance venues as existed anywhere else in the country. From underground punk clubs to metal clubs to dance clubs to small theaters to lavish amphitheaters— even a baseball stadium— pretty much every kind of performance space was available for bands in Orange County, all with the exception of an indoor arena to rival the size and space of places like the Forum in Los Angeles and Madison Square Garden in New York. But early into the next decade, that would change.

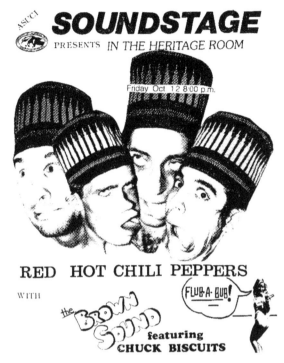

This ad is from when the Red Hot Chili Peppers performed at UC Irvine. *Author's collection.*

And as tastes and trends continued to evolve, Orange County would again become a hotbed of new bands. In suburban garages all over the county, bands had witnessed what happened with groups like No Doubt and the Offspring. They had also seen the crash and burn realities of many punk bands like Social Distortion and China White. But the bottom line was, young bands all understood that Orange County was a highly fertile launching pad for whatever your rock 'n' roll dreams were, as long as you were willing to work for it.

Chapter 5

THE 1990s

The club that today bears the name the Observatory in Costa Mesa has a very interesting history. The building opened in 1974 and was called the Harlequin Dinner Playhouse. Dinner theater was a hugely popular form of entertainment around the country in the 1980s but especially in Orange County, and thus the 450-seat performance space hosted many popular shows. In 1989, it morphed into a restaurant-concert space called Hamptons and, for two years, booked a fairly solid roster of touring acts, including David Johansen, the former New York Doll frontman who was then touring with an alter-ego act called Buster Poindexter, as well as bands such as Blood, Sweat and Tears. Hamptons closed down in 1990, and in the same space, the Rhythm Café opened in 1992. The Rhythm Café was, by design, supposed to morph into a national chain of concert clubs, something along the lines of what the House of Blues would do soon afterward. However, the concept never really got off the ground, and within a year, the Galaxy Concert Theater opened. Opened by Gary Folgner, the man who launched the Coach House in San Juan Capistrano, the Galaxy did well compared to previous tenants. From 1993 until 2008, artists as diverse as Jimmy Cliff, Beck and Lucinda Williams all performed there. Next came the Revolver, which was intended to be a high-end restaurant/nightclub. However, the city of Santa Ana never gave the approval for a nightclub to open there, and so Revolver never got off the ground at all. Folgner then returned and reopened the Galaxy from 2009 to 2011. Since then, it has become the

THE 1990s

Observatory, a rock 'n' roll club that still books everybody from Cheap Trick to Jonathan Richman to Gary Newman.

Another club that attracted a lot of attention in the early '90s was the Bandstand in Anaheim. Of all the hard-core and metal shows that took place there in the early 1990s, many fans remember when Pantera played there in May 1991 during the *Cowboys from Hell* tour.

With the early 1990s came more homegrown bands in Orange County, including the Aquabats, a comedic rock outfit formed in Brea. Christian Jacobs, Chad Larson and Boyd Terry had all been playing in various Orange County alternative and punk bands and then came up with the idea of forming a band to satirize the well-known Orange County punk scene. In the middle of this idea, Jacobs was also taken in by the growing ska scene in Orange County and liked the fact that it was less aggressive and more musical. This observation affected the concept of the band, and soon, with Larson playing bass, Jacobs singing lead vocals and Terry on the trumpet, the Aquabats began developing their sound, which would ultimately include punk, ska, surf and a number of other elements.

They also tapped into the idea of matching band costumes after having been inspired by Devo. In fact, their band concept evolved into literally a cross between Devo and surf music. The three original members started incorporating several other musicians, including a full horn section. In the mid-1990s, the band costumes ranged from chefs outfits to wearing skirts, but once the members came into a large surplus of spare rubber and neoprene, they designed a set of unique helmets, rash guards vinyl belts and other uniform parts that gave them a look of underwater superheroes. Next they began adopting superhero names and created a full storyline to go along with their own made-up mythology. Their debut album came out in 1996. Entitled the *Return of the Aquabats*, it was a do-it-yourself venture that still managed to sell around twenty thousand copies, a very impressive first self-release. As the popularity of ska music grew, thanks to groups like No Doubt, Sublime and Reel Big Fish, the Aquabats became more popular as well. They signed a recording contract in 1996 and began touring the country extensively. In 1997, one of their drummers was Travis Barker. The next year, in the middle of a tour with pop punk legends Blink-182, Blink-182 fired its drummer, Scott Raynor, and invited Barker to sit in for the last of the series of shows.

By the end of the tour, Blink-182 was so impressed with Barker that he was brought on as a full-time member. The Aquabats are still together today, and while there have been many other personnel changes over the years, they still managed to put on an entertaining show with full costumes and comedic skits.

Around the same time that the Aquabats were getting started, another band had begun making music in Huntington Beach. Originally from Bakersfield, Korn relocated to Orange County in 1993 and rented a local studio in Huntington Beach called Underground Chicken Sound. The band began playing around Orange County, including regular gigs in Huntington Beach at Club 5902, the original site of Night Moves. While sharing a house in town, the band was spotted by an Epic Records A&R man named Paul Pontious. In Korn, Pontious heard something wildly different and provocative, a darkly ferocious and rhythmic musical concoction that would soon earn the term "nu metal."

Led by frontman Jonathan Davis, in 1993, Korn released its initial demo entitled *Niedermayer's Mind*. Though there were not many of them printed, the album was influential enough to attract even more attention. In 1994, the band began recording its debut album, and on October 11, this self-titled debut was released on Immortal Records. All of a sudden, nu metal had been truly born. The record was reasonably successful, and Korn's next release, 1996's *Life Is Peachy*, was far more of a hit, being certified two times platinum in the United States with big sales in other countries as well. "No Place to Hide," which was the first single, garnered a Grammy nomination for Best Metal Performance for Korn.

But the real mainstream breakthrough happened with Korn's third album, entitled *Follow the Leader*. The band had recruited a number of guest vocalists on the album, including Ice Cube and actor Cheech Marin. It debuted at number one on the *Billboard* 200, and the song "Freak on a Leash" won a Grammy for Best Music Video as well as nine MTV Video Music Award nominations.

Since starting out in Huntington Beach, Korn has gone on to become one of the most commercially and critically acclaimed bands of its generation. As Davis said about the early days:

> *Huntington Beach was a really great place for us. Coming from Bakersfield, which is really dry and dusty, it was a refreshing change. Bakersfield will always be home and we'll always love it there and we'll always have lots of family and friends there. But the scene down in Orange County was [what] we needed at that time. It's where we really developed as a band and played some of our best early shows right there in Huntington Beach. It will always be an important place for Korn, and I'm not sure*

Jonathan Davis was the lead singer of the band Korn, whose members signed their first record deal while living in Huntington Beach. *Courtesy of Charles Epting.*

our band would've even been discovered the way it was were not for us living there.

In the years after Korn's career erupted, their former drummer David Silvera opened a sushi bar in Huntington Beach called Tuna Town.

In the early 1990s, business at the Irvine Meadows amphitheater was as busy as ever, still packing the house and the giant lawn area for dozens of shows, including the Dave Matthews Band, David Bowie, Rush and Jimmy Buffett. But bands like Green Day, Blink-182 and Tool were also filling the amphitheater. All of a sudden, a lot of the late '80s and early '90s punk and alternative bands had begun finding major commercial success.

In 1993, Orange County lost one of its primary heavy metal music venues. Jezebels, which was located at 125 North State College Boulevard in Anaheim, had opened in 1986 and served as kind of a training ground for young Orange County hard rock and heavy metal bands that wanted to earn their chops before venturing outside the county. But the club was also visited by such legendary metal acts as Armored Saint, Megadeth and even

Metallica. Once the grunge movement started hitting in the early '90s, the end was near for clubs such as Jezebels. Fans and musicians still remember the club fondly and stage the occasional get-together in honor of the former metal palace.

In the midst of all this, Orange County finally got an arena to fill the last missing piece in the rock 'n' roll performance venue puzzle.

The Arrowhead Pond opened up in Anaheim right near Anaheim Stadium on June 19, 1993. The headlining act to open the building was Barry Manilow. The all-purpose arena has been home to the Mighty Ducks hockey team since opening while hosting dozens of other sporting events. But it also fills the void of being able to attract touring arena bands that would normally only play up in Los Angeles and perhaps in San Diego when in Southern California. Since opening, the arena, which is now called the Honda Center, has hosted dozens of the biggest acts in the world.

Gwen Stephani filmed a pair of solo concerts here in 2005.

Depeche Mode has performed at the arena six times, and U-2 has played at the arena five times. The Rolling Stones, Fleetwood Mac, Kiss, Rush and Blink-182 have all performed at the arena.

At this point in time, if music fans chose to never leave Orange County, they would still be able to see as many, if not more, bands than in any other region in the United States.

Yet another Orange County rock band emerged on the scene in 1998. Thrice hailed from the city of Irvine and was founded by guitarist/vocalist Dustin Kensrue and guitarist Teppei Teranishi while they were still in high school. Originally known for fast-paced rock created by heavily distorted guitar sounds and wildly imaginative and complex time signatures, Thrice self-released an EP in 1999 entitled *First Impressions*. The band pressed just one thousand copies and hustled them from out of their cars. Within a year, they had recorded another dozen tracks and then released *Identity Crisis* on Green Flag Records. The proggy, post-hard-core band finally attracted the attention of Orange County–based Hopeless Records, which released *The Illusion of Safety* in 2002. The band continued releasing records, and uniquely, each record saw part of its proceeds donated to a different charity. Since starting out, Thrice has long been a favorite of critics.

This is a portion of an absolutepunk.net review for the 2012 Thrice effort *Major/Minor*:

> *Whereas most bands have that one album that define a career, Thrice continuously reinforced their ever building legacy with one champion*

after the next without sticking to a tried and tested formula and without succumbing to pressure to write a "hit." Message board discussions about Thrice always bring up the what is their best album debate and what is striking time and time again is that every list has all eight of their albums in completely different orders; proof of an exceptional catalog. Thrice have spanned more genres, concepts and themes than most bands have managed over the last 10 years put together. One would think this would exert enormous amounts of pressure on them every time they release a new album—but the anticipation of a Thrice album is really a question of how good it will be. The trust displayed by their fans has, for the most part, always been exemplary, creating a passionate following."

Following the 2012 spring tour, Thrice went on hiatus with plans to return at some point in the future.

As the 1990s came to a close, the stage was set for one of Orange County's biggest musical stories to take root. It would result in one of the biggest modern bands of the decade, but as always, there were more bands and more venues to follow.

Chapter 6
THE 2000s

I n May 2009, I wrote the following article for the *Huntington Beach Independent* newspaper:

On the back window of a vehicle parked on a well-kept street in a neighborhood near Central Library, there is a sticker for the band Avenged Sevenfold. While you'd be right in assuming that the vehicle belongs to a big fan, which fan might surprise you. It's not one of the millions of high school or college kids who have helped make this innovative, intense metal band one of the hottest in the world right now. Rather, the vehicle belongs to Joe Sullivan, the drummer's dad.

Joe and Barbara Sullivan, who have lived in the same comfortable Huntington Beach house since 1977, may not look like rock 'n' roll parents. Spend some time with them, though, and you'll realize how deceptive looks can be. Since their son Jim (a.k.a. "The Rev") hit it big (literally and figuratively) with Avenged Sevenfold, they've become industry experts.

They can just as easily discuss the importance of merchandise sales as they can the financial implications of headlining a gig versus being an opening act—and most importantly, they love the music. Raising their son, 28, in this house along with sisters Kelly and Katie, they knew early on that Jim's life might involve percussion.

"He was desperately into music," Joe says, laughing. "In the bathtub when he was tiny he'd be banging away on things. Then, pots and pans—anything and everything."

THE 2000S

Avenged Sevenfold drummer Jimmy Sullivan (far left) with his family in Huntington Beach.
Courtesy of the Sullivan family.

Barbara adds, "So finally we got him a little drum kit from Sears. And we knew—we just knew this was serious."

Neither of his folks are musicians, so Jim's mom went to a music store that used to be at Warner Avenue and Springdale Street when he was about 6. There, they met Jeanette Raitt, a teacher who became very influential and helped spark his passion for complex percussive challenges. Soon, the young drummer discovered Metallica, then Pantera.

"Faster and faster stuff," Joe says. "And his teacher had him transcribing all the drum work so he could really understand what was happening."

When Jim was 10, his folks got him a more serious drum kit—an old Ludwig set with lots of cymbals.

"When his teacher found out he'd been figuring out the parts on a little toy set, she was amazed," says Barbara.

Jim played with several local bands including Suburban Legends, before finding his way into Avenged Sevenfold, who formed about 10 years ago, in high school. All five band members (M. Shadows, vocals; Zacky Vengeance, guitar; Synyster Gates, guitar; Johnny Christ, bass; and Jim "The Rev" Sullivan, Drums) hail from Huntington Beach.

Supposedly, the band's name refers to the book of "Genesis" in the Bible and the story of Cain and Abel, where Cain is punished to live in exile, alone and miserable. Anyone who relieved Cain of his misery by killing him would be "avenged in sevenfold," or punished in a way that is seven times worse than Cain's punishment. However, M. Shadows, the driving force and de facto band leader, has stated in interviews that the band is not "not really religious at all."

After forming, they released the album "Sounding the Seventh Trumpet." Their follow-up album, "Waking the Fallen," broadened their fan base quickly, and critical acclaim was swift:

Rolling Stone: "These guys excel at the complex, pummeling Eighties-metal moves that first came into circulation when they were in diapers."

Spin magazine: "A Godzilla-size pileup of whiplash metalcore and Sunset Strip swagger, Avenged Sevenfold's 2005 major-label debut, 'City of Evil,' won unexpected platinum status."

Blender: "Avenged Sevenfold transcended the headbanger heartland with 2005's 'Bat Country.' Its mixture of campy goth and '80s Sunset Strip debauchery was matched with a refreshing sound that fused florid guitar solos with frenzied nail-gun drumming, while M. Shadows shifted effortlessly between a snarl and a croon."

And 2007's "Avenged Sevenfold" album won the Kerrang! Awards Best Album award in 2008. Joe and Barbara have watched their son learn to live on his own, as a member of an up-and-coming band that would soon be touring the world.

"It wasn't that easy at first," Barbara explains. "Those first tours, like the first 'Warped Tour,' they'd be in a van driving all night, not eating right. But they learned discipline fast, and the importance of hard work. These young guys work very hard."

Today, the families of the band know each other and it's a very close-knit bunch in the Avenged organization. Crewmembers went to grade school with the band, the musicians are all high school buddies—and it all happened here in Huntington.

The Sullivans are amazed with their son's life and support every beat of it. "We love to hear how the music evolves when they're working on it," Joe says, smiling. "We love the shows, the feedback from fans and family members—it's an incredible experience."

Barbara scrapbooks many of her son's musical moments and also collects much of the band's memorabilia, including lunch boxes, watches and coasters. She also remembers what it was like when all three kids were home.

"While Jimmy played drums, his sister Kelly was playing classical music on French horn, and his other sister Katie would paint—there was always wonderful art being created around us."

Mom's favorite show to date? "A long time ago, right as they started catching on, up at the Ford Theater in Los Angeles. Jimmy still says that they weren't that good yet, but watching the kids in the crowd sing along to every song—you knew something special was happening." She pulls out the MTV "spaceman" statue that the band won as Best New Artist at the 2006 MTV Video Music Awards as proof of how right she was.

And what does Joe feel when he watches the band play live today before thousands of adoring fans?

"I look at him up there under the lights, and I think back to the little kid in the tub; that little boy hitting those toys together. It's incredible to think about what he has done and where he's been. But you know, it doesn't just happen. He worked so hard—all these guys work so hard, and that's that thing I think people should realize. They're great because of the time they put in. How can you not be proud of that?"

By that time, Avenged Sevenfold has firmly established itself as an intense and dynamic hard rock band. They first formed in 1999, lead vocalist M. Shadows, guitarists Zacky Vengeance and Synyster Gates, drummer Jimmy Sullivan and bassist Matt Wendt (later replaced by Justin Sane). The band cut

M. Shadows was the lead singer for Huntington Beach–based Avenged Sevenfold. *Author's collection.*

two demos in 1999 and 2000 and after a series of personnel changes finally arrived with bass player Johnny Christ before releasing their second studio album entitled "Waking the Fallen" in 2003. Now on the Hopeless Records label, they hit the road on the Van's Warped Tour among several other high profile tours. Signing with Warner Bros. Records, they next released "City of Evil" in 2005 and it sold 30,000 copies in its first week of release.

They played Ozzfest in 2006 [and] also won the best new artist award at the MTV music video awards. The band's dramatic themes and darkly personal lyrics [won] them fiercely dedicated and loyal fan base from very early on. Their next release, a 2007 self-titled effort won them even more fans as they moved further away from their death metal roots into a more mainstream form of metal that still managed to embrace all the emotion and heaviness of their earlier efforts.

Then, on the heels of what would become a major breakthrough in the form of their first number one album, tragedy struck. On December 28, 2009, Jimmy Sullivan was found dead at his home in Huntington Beach. Original autopsy reveals results were inconclusive, but six months later the cause of death was revealed to have been intoxication [due] to combined effects of a variety of prescription drugs.

Though the band originally considered disbanding due to the loss of their musical brother, in February 2010 they returned to the studio with the then-Dream Theater drummer Mike Portnoy filling in for Sullivan. Portnoy had been one of Sullivan's idols and once he reached out to the band [to] offer his condolences following Solomon's death, discussions took place that eventually resulted in Portnoy filling in for the fallen drummer. Once the album, entitled "Nightmare" was released in July 2010, Portnoy went on the road with the band to fill in on the Nightmare tour. By the end of the year, Portnoy left the band and they eventually settled on drummer Arin Illejay as Sullivan's full-time replacement.

In 2012, Avenged Sevenfold won the award for Best Live Band and Most Dedicated Fans at the Revolver Golden Gods awards. Touring around the world relentlessly, their fan base just became stronger and stronger. On August 27, 2013 their album "Hail to the King" revealed a more classic and mature metal sound for A7X, as they are known.

As critically acclaimed as anything they've ever released, the album also hit number one on the charts establishing the band as one of the true worldwide powerhouse bands.

While Orange County had produced a host of hard rock stars over the years from Dave Mustaine to Scott Weiland, Avenged Sevenfold was the first true metal band to emerge exclusively from Orange County to achieve the heights they had reached.

For many fans though, both in Orange County and all over the world, the loss of Sullivan remains an integral part of the band's identity and legacy. The funeral held for Sullivan several days after his death was attended by many musical artists [including] members of My Chemical Romance and Buckcherry. It was a rock 'n' roll funeral unlike anything else that had never been witnessed in Orange County.

Being friends with the Sullivan family [m]y family and I attended the funeral and I was given permission to write about it afterwards [for] my newspaper column. What follows here was the only published account of the poignant event.

I'm sitting here trying to make sense and write this column about what I witnessed last week—the two services I attended for Jimmy "The Rev" Sullivan, drummer (who wrote and sang) for the Huntington Beach–based band Avenged Sevenfold. If you saw the column I wrote a few months back about Joe and Barbara Sullivan, Jimmy's parents, you'll remember that this tight-knit family knew early that the little boy banging on toys in the tub was destined for something percussive—but as the member of a spectacularly popular band?

The gravesite in Huntington Beach of Jimmy "the Rev" Sullivan, the original drummer for Avenged Sevenfold. *Courtesy of Charles Epting.*

"The Rev" tragically passed away at 28 the week before last, and while nobody is quite sure what happened, it really doesn't matter—what's important is that a family here misses their son (and brother). Joe and Barbara Sullivan want to address the fans soon, and they will. For now, not as a columnist but as a friend, I asked their permission to convey the power of what I witnessed at the services, and they said it was OK. But as I sit here, it's hard to know where to begin.

This lovely family (including Jimmy's sisters Kelly and Katie) was visible at the services not just gracefully tending to the assembled flock, but on the several scrapbook photo boards at the church featuring hundreds of family photos. Vacations, camping trips, birthdays, ball games, Jimmy playing one of his first sets of drums—they all grew up right before our eyes. So how do you begin to write of the vastness of this loss the family is feeling? I can tell you that as friends and family paid tribute to The Rev at the rosary service the night before the funeral, it was powerful, heartfelt and real—just like The Rev himself. The packed church was treated to stories from pals, relatives and his first drum teacher, who spoke of the young boy who understood and executed polyrhythmic theory in a matter of weeks. Grade-school buddies recalled the happy-go-lucky athlete who became a real-life rock star but never forget where he came from. The four remaining members of Avenged Sevenfold entered together and then rose together to address the crowd.

Tearfully, these young men, wives and girlfriends by their side[s], shared their love of their band mate. Finally, The Rev's dad, Joe Sullivan, spoke about his son, honoring him with an eloquent speech on how much he learned from his boy—and how it will affect his life going forward. There was pain in the room, but it was trumped by joy and love generated by The Rev, whom many felt comfortable, justifiably, in calling their best friend. The funeral the next day was an equally dramatic, beautiful event. In addition to the hundreds of family and friends gathered (including Jimmy's fiancée, Leana), there were several bands in attendance, including members of Buckcherry and My Chemical Romance. Flowers, cymbals and drumheads signed by legendary bands were delivered—representing the love and respect among the band's brethren. Avenged Sevenfold guitarist Brian Haner, a.k.a. Synyster Gates, delivered a soaring eulogy with focus and class.

You look at him and the other young men in the band, M. Shadows, Zacky Vengeance and Johnny Christ, and wonder what they must be feeling—but in their eyes, you see the pain of their loss. I will tell you here

THE 2000s

that besides their music, what I love about Avenged Sevenfold is that they choose to remain part of Huntington Beach. They could easily have left after hitting it big, but they didn't. They bought homes here, they're known around town, they hire their buddies as crew; they're good guys. Rock stars? Whatever. They're hard-working, successful young men who got where they are because they're very good at what they do, and the city is better for having them here. Back to the Sullivan family. As they clung together at the church and at the cemetery, surrounded by hundreds of mourners, it reminded one that the son they gave the world affected many lives—young lives. As I struggled trying to write this column, an e-mail arrived. It was from a young woman in Omaha, Neb., Rachel Lee. She's a 22-year-old librarian who loves Avenged Sevenfold. Her note read in part, "I specifically wanted to thank you for humanizing the drummer and his family, giving a sense of what those of us who have looked up at their stage and sung their lyrics, begged for their autographs, have only sensed at a distance—that at the end of the night their loved ones back in Huntington Beach are truly their family and their home.

"While the fandom has suffered a great loss, we dearly wish to express that they are not alone in their grief and there are a lot of us out there who wish we could do something to ease the pain of Jimmy's passing. Tonight, a candlelight vigil is being planned in a number of cities in his memory, fans gathering together to talk and laugh and remember The Rev." She went on to tell me about a scrapbook project in honor of Jimmy being headed by a young woman in Florida, Victoria Deroy, who also wrote to express her sorrow over Jimmy's loss, and her plan to help keep his memory alive. "Avenged Sevenfold saved my life, and from the moment I heard of Jimmy's death, I felt as though my entire world had fallen apart," she wrote. "I wanted to comfort the men that I had grown to know and love through their music, DVDs and live performances. I sent out over 20 messages to fan pages and tried to get several of my friends involved and the end result was over 190 messages from fans all over the world. We received prayers, notes and stories, even from people who had known Jimmy personally. I am currently in the process of hand-crafting the scrapbook and will send it out as soon as I am finished."

Losses like this will never be easy for me to process, make sense of and write about, but the words of these fans brought some clarity. Jimmy's loss is being felt by millions all around the world—especially by a family and a band of brothers here in Huntington Beach. If you haven't listened to Avenged Sevenfold, I recommend you do. It's raw, passionate music played with skill, soul and unbridled fury. My 16-year-old son, Charlie, adores this band, so we have had the benefit of hearing them constantly—as I write this, their song "Critical Acclaim" plays loudly, and proudly, behind me. Listen to the music, listen to the magic, and by all means, listen to the backbeat thunder. There's no way better way to honor the Sullivan family—after all, that's their boy on the drums."

To date, the gravesite of Jimmy Sullivan is a regular stopping point for Avenged Sevenfold fans from all over the world. These were just a few of the hundreds of notes from fans in response to the articles that I wrote in Orange County. The effect of his loss was simply stunning.

These remembrances document just how far the influence of a drummer from Huntington Beach spanned:

My very own forlorn and somber nightmare was shockingly manifested on Dec. 28, a day considered by many to be unluckiest day of the year. To the Sullivans, Leana and the rest of the A7X family: Jimmy will never be forgotten by those that saw him for the talented, loving and carefree genius that he was—my heart aches for you each and every day.

—Joelle, Bella Vista, Alaska

I will never forget Jimmy "The Rev" Sullivan. Although I never met him, he showed me how to truly live life to the fullest.

—Hunter, Yorba Linda, California

Jimmy Sullivan touched my life in such an amazing way, and I never even got to meet him. I didn't have to.

—Ashley, Albuquerque, New Mexico

A musical genius, but more importantly a mover of souls. Thank you for allowing us a glimpse into your beautiful heart and foREVer changing our lives.

—Sherri Miller, Heavener, Oklahoma

I feel terribly sorry that you've lost Jimmy one year ago. We will pray for you today, from all over the world.

—Lean, Holland

THE 2000s

From the opening riffs of "To End the Rapture" to the last notes of "Save Me" and everything in between, Jimmy "The Rev" Sullivan has been a songwriting hero and inspiration to me.

—Tom, Atlantic City, New Jersey

Jimmy was a perfect chapter in our lives. Stay strong Sullivans.

—Hanna Salmela, Finland

Sullivans, I wish you could know just how much your son and his band mean to me. It was an honour and a dream come true to be there at Sonisphere 2009 to witness The Rev play his last show.

—Hayley, Bexhill-On-Sea, England

Every day without Jimmy is a challenge, but even now he helps us through the tough times. He'll never be forgotten by those whose hearts he touched.

—Renee, Sydney, Australia

Thank you, from the bottom of my heart, for giving us one of the greatest drummers of this generation. He will be foREVer missed.

—Paulina Castillo, Los Angeles, California

Jimmy and his music still bring a smile to the faces of those who watch and hear him play. A true legend and funny bloke!

—Lew, Wolverhampton, England

A huge thanks to the Sullivan family who let Jimmy share his amazing gift with the world. His legacy will never be forgotten.

—Charlhynn D., Spokane, Washington

A year ago today, the world lost a special man, and from that day forward, Jimmy's fans made a promise to keep his legacy alive foREVer. We've kept true to that promise, and we only hope that our efforts have shone bright enough to lead you, his family, through the toughest of times. We love you.

—Arielle, Westminster, England

The death doesn't mean the end. How long we will remember about Jimmy, he will live forever. FoREVer in our hearts.

—Natka, Poland

Another Huntington Beach band started finding its way around the time that Avenged Sevenfold first formed. "One of the Best New Bands of 2010"—that's what *Rolling Stone* said about the Dirty Heads.

The band, which has actually been around in various forms since 1996, sums itself up in an official bio: "Rooted in the Orange County community of Huntington Beach, the Dirty Heads emerged onto the Southern California music scene with their unique signature blend of acoustic infused hip-hop and classic reggae, creating the perfect soundtrack to an upbeat, sun-soaked California."

Along with Avenged Sevenfold, the Dirty Heads also put focus on Huntington as a musical mecca in the early 2000s, and lead singer Jared Watson likes that his band is now often spoken about in the same sentence with his Surf City brethren.

"We went to Marina High; they went to Huntington. But we knew each other well growing up," Watson said. "They're awesome guys. In fact, my best friend growing up was Jimmy Sullivan."

The Dirty Heads, though much different in sound from Avenged Sevenfold, have managed to carve out their own international success while still remaining firmly rooted in Orange County.

"This is our home; this is where we will always be from," said Watson. "We learned everything about music right here in this beach town, and we like to think other bands can look at us and say, You know what, it's not impossible. You can still make music and survive."

Also formed around 1999 in Orange County was Atreyu, a metal-core band named after a character from the fantasy book *The Neverending Story*. Led by vocalist Alex Varkatzas, guitarists Dan Jacobs and Travis Miguel, bassist Marc McKnight and drummer-vocalist Brandon Saller, the band's first full-length album, entitled *Suicide Notes and Butterfly Kisses*, was released in 2001 by Victory Records. Right away, the release captured a large audience, in part thanks to a video for the song "Lip Gloss and Black," which achieved a lot of airplay on MTV's *Headbangers Ball 2003*. The big breakthrough came in 2004 when the trio released *The Curse*. It sold almost half a million copies, and soon after, the band was featured on the soundtrack to the film *Mr. & Mrs. Smith* when it covered the Bon Jovi smash-hit "You Give Love a Bad Name." Over the years, Atreyu continued to release powerful records, but in 2011, the band stopped working together. Instead, all the members began pursuing individual projects. Then in the summer of 2014, word got out that the band would soon be resuming its career together with a series of shows later in the year. It was huge news for

THE 2000s

Brandon Saller (left) and Dan Jacobs from Atreyu. *Courtesy of Charles Epting*

this Orange County band and the more than one million Facebook fans it
had amassed over the years.

Upon the announcement, Brandon Saller had this to say:

> *Discussions probably began about eight months ago. We all had dinner one
> night in Huntington Beach and figured out that we had an urge to make
> more music. It was that simple. We talked about some options, and things
> grew really fast. Back then, we all decided it was kind of pointless to be in
> a band if we weren't all going to be 110%. When you're in a band, that's
> just how it has to be. I hate to see a band up there that is starting to phone
> it in. I feel ripped off. We didn't want to get to that point, but we knew that
> possibly we were heading down that road. We had no idea what the reaction
> would be, so we didn't want to think about it too much. We just want to
> get together and start kicking around some music. But then it hit us like a
> tidal wave. The reaction has been insane. On the one hand, we never really
> knew what people thought of us, but then again we look at our Facebook
> page, which had about 500,000 likes right before the hiatus. We haven't
> done anything in a few years, and yet now I think it's over about a million
> and a half. I never really looked at that before, but when you think about it,
> I guess people do really care about this band.*

And Dan Jacobs offered:

I think it's clear that we have some unfinished business. When we went on hiatus four years ago, we didn't know if we would be back. When you're in a band as long as we had been, it's interesting because we started [as] teenagers. You go through those years together living in Never Neverland, and you never really grow up. We just got to a point where we wanted to see what we are made of outside of being in a band. We wanted to establish ourselves be individuals and now we can go back a little bit older and wiser and get back to business.

In January 2001, a former punk rock legend died in Orange County. Bryan Gregory, a founding member of and guitarist for the Cramps drove himself to the emergency room at Anaheim Memorial Medical Center in the middle of the night after feeling exhausted and ill. Suddenly and quite unexpectedly, he suffered a multiple-systems failure at the hospital and passed away there. While he was not from Orange County, Gregory's former band, the Cramps, had played in the county numerous times.

Around the same time that Avenged Sevenfold and Atreyu started performing, a small club in a dingy little strip mall in Anaheim also opened its doors. This is how the *OC Weekly* describes Chain Reaction:

Remember when you were 17 and all you wanted to do was to be able to see your favorite band that never played any all-ages venue? EVER? Well the Chain Reaction solves all that. This is like the introductory venue for every band that passes through Orange County—everyone's played the Chain at some point in their careers. It's a small, slightly dingy venue located in a sketchy Anaheim shopping center surrounded by car dealerships. The floors are sticky, the stage is small, dusty T-shirts of bands that have played the venue grace the walls and any space that's free is covered in bumper stickers. But since when was rock and roll ever clean? This place is a no-fuss, straight to the point venue where covers are cheap and indie bands are frequent. Everyone wins.

Since opening, Chain Reaction has become one of the most vital punk venues in the country. The intimate space and all-ages policy allows for typically intense shows on many nights, and the place remains a throwback to other glory days clubs like the Cuckoo's Nest and Safari Sam's.

Many big local bands, such as Avenged Sevenfold and Atreyu, played there on the way up, but many other bands did as well, including My

Chemical Romance and Coheed and Cambria, among others. It's a no-frills and nothing-fancy environment with lots of band T-shirts tacked up on the walls. Chain Reaction has proven itself to be one of the most consistently dependable venues for punk, pop punk and other related musical subgenres. I've spoken to many bands that played over the years, and without fail, they all talk about the place in glowing and legendary terms. Tons of kids grew up listening to bootleg tapes from this small club and eventually went off and formed their own bands.

In 1998, adjacent to the parking lot at Anaheim Stadium, a Hollywood-themed restaurant named Tinseltown Studios opened up. That concept failed, however, and the building was renamed the Sun Theater in 1999 when concerts began being held in the 1,700-seat venue. In 2001, it was renamed the Grove and, since then, has become a popular place for big-name artists looking for an intimate venue. Everyone from Bob Dylan to B.B. King to Ice Cube has performed there over the years, and in a sense, the Grove fills a void once occupied by the Anaheim Convention Center Arena (which still exists but rarely hosts concerts any more).

And the new high-profile venues did not stop there. In 2001, a House of Blues opened at Downtown Disney and today continues to attract a wide variety of performers.

Also in the 2000s, the Rolling Stones returned to Anaheim Stadium in both 2002 and 2005. U2 also returned to Anaheim to play the stadium in 2011. And Irvine Meadows Amphitheater, now rechristened the Verizon Wireless Amphitheater, remains just as busy as ever.

In 2006, at the former site of a small Fullerton café known as the Hub, the Slidebar Rock 'n Roll Kitchen opened. What's most impressive about this place, next to the fact that it regularly has good local bands playing, is how it embraces the history of Orange County music. Of course, one reason might be its location: the parking lot is exactly where Leo Fender created the Stratocaster, the Telecaster and many other iconic guitars.

From tiny and vital clubs, such as Chain Reaction, all the way through to a venue like Angel Stadium, Orange County in the 2000s featured just about as broad a variety of musical venues as any other county in the United States.

Tragedy struck on Halloween night 2012 in Huntington Beach when Mitch Lucker, lead singer of the band Suicide Silence, was killed after crashing his motorcycle into a lamppost not far from where he lived with his wife and young daughter. At a vigil the next night at the crash site, Lucker's wife, Jolie, said to a crowd of grief-stricken fans, "He was an

This makeshift memorial is at the site where Mitch Lucker, lead singer of Suicide Silence, was killed in Huntington Beach in 2012. *Author's collection.*

alcoholic, and it's been a big battle. I tried to stop him. I was in front of him begging him not to leave the house. Begging him. 'Just seriously, for us, don't leave.' And he did. And this is what happened…He was an amazing man. He was a wonderful father and a great husband. And now he's gonna miss out on watching Kenadee grow, because he decided to drink and ride."

In 2011, video footage emerged that claimed to be the very first ever Rage Against the Machine concert. Shot with a shaky hand-held camera, the footage captured the band playing a college show at Cal State Northridge outside Los Angeles. But as band member Tom Morello commented when he saw the footage:

> *I have seen a bit of* [the] *clip, and I have a full recollection of that show. It was actually the first time we played in front of a public audience; we had done one show previously, but that was a living room party. So that filmed footage still qualifies as our first 'proper' show. I remember when we started playing there was no one in the audience, it was just people walking back and forward on the way to lunch at Cal State Northridge. After an hour-long performance, we won over a couple of headbangers, which was a victory for us at that point in our careers!*

THE 2000s

As a band bio notes:

Rage Against the Machine (also Rage and RATM) is an American rock band, noted for their blend of hip hop, heavy metal, punk and funk as well as their revolutionary politics and lyrics. During their initial nine-year run, they became one of the most popular and influential political bands in contemporary music.

In 1991, guitarist Tom Morello left his old band, Lock Up, looking to start another band. Morello was in a club in L.A. where Zack de la Rocha was free-style rapping. Morello was impressed by de la Rocha's lyric books, and asked him to be the vocalist in a band. Morello called and drafted drummer Brad Wilk, who had previously auditioned for Lock Up, while de la Rocha convinced his childhood friend Tim Commerford to join as bassist.

Shortly after forming, they gave their first public performance in Orange County, California, where a friend of Commerford's was holding a house party.

That's right, the living room party show Morello mentions also took place somewhere in Orange County. Many have tried to track the exact location, but to date, the efforts have come up short.

It certainly makes one wonder about what *don't* we know about the music history of Orange County. There will always be rumors about supposed sightings and sessions that may or may not have taken place here. But no matter what, enough has happened here that certainly makes Orange County a musical mecca. It's not possible to cover the complete musical history of the county in one simple book. There are many books that could easily be written just about the punk scene in Orange County. From Social Distortion to T.S.O.L. to the Vandals and on and on, it is almost unfathomable the amount of compelling musical rebellion this county has produced.

For more than sixty-five years now, rock 'n' roll has been being made in Orange County. In a small house in Santa Ana, the Rillera family started a band that connected with many people, fans and musicians alike, and acted as a catalyst for much of what happen throughout the county in the 1950s. It all started in a garage in that house, and although the home is long gone, the effects of the music those brothers made in there is still felt.

All of the late '70s punk bands throughout Orange County are connected to that family home. The spirit of strapping on a guitar and letting the world know you are here may seem like a simple thing today, but it was revolutionary back then. This was before Elvis and the Beatles and Chuck Berry.

For all the clichés about Orange County being sleepy and suburban and nothing more than a hotbed of conservative politics, the music tells a much different story. In beach towns and in the suburbs alike, there exists a sense of freedom and opportunity that has clearly inspired many musicians in the area.

Kids growing up in Orange County from the 1960s on never suffered for lack of being able to see live music. I can't tell you how many musicians I've interviewed in my career as a journalist who talk about sneaking into the Golden Bear or hopping fences at the old Irvine Meadows Amphitheater to catch a show for free. It was a much different county when Led Zeppelin first visited here in 1969, and I wonder if Jimmy Page and Robert Plant had any memory of those early shows in Anaheim and UC Irvine when they came back to Irvine to play together at Irvine Meadows many years later.

Many bands that I have interviewed over the years that played the Anaheim Convention Center Arena and other venues back in the '60s and '70s have mentioned the fact that playing in Orange County was typically a more loose and more fun experience than performing up in Los Angeles. You didn't have the press breathing down your neck, there tended to be fewer industry people and the crowds were not as jaded. These were just fans who were thrilled to see you, and they let you know it when you came out.

Arguably the most vital musical element to have ever existed in Orange County was the punk rock movement of the late '70s and early '80s. It seemed so unexpected to many that a place as placid and laid-back could produce such anger and raw honesty. And that's why it matters so much. Because the music of bands like Social Distortion and the Vandals changed how people thought about Orange County. They proved once and for all that it didn't matter where you came from—if you were pissed off and energized and motivated and wanted to start a band that could change the world, you could do it. In fact the lethargy and clichés that kids were fighting back against in Orange County probably helped drive a lot of the intensity. Artists can be born anywhere, and if the place where they exist inspires them to want to shake things up, well, that's probably when you start getting bands like T.S.O.L.

Music has changed since the 1960s. Radio no longer plays much of a force in making music popular. Records and CDs are museum artifacts. But it doesn't matter. On any given night of the week, if a club like Chain Reaction can be packed with a couple hundred sweaty, moshing, crazed fans who are living in the moment, singing every word to every song, then the system is working. Because that's all it will ever be about. Live music played by real bands for fans who care. Thankfully, it seems Orange County will always have places like that, which means the bands will always come here.

But even bigger than that, the success of bands such as Avenged Sevenfold and Korn remind the up-and-coming musician that no matter how much the business changes, you've always got a shot.

CONCLUDING THOUGHTS FROM BARRY RILLERA

B arry Rillera, whose story is detailed elsewhere in this book, was for three decades associated with the Righteous Brothers as lead guitarist, bandleader and tour manager. An Orange County music legend, he also toured with Ray Charles and White Trash.

> *Orange County has always produced good musicians. At least, that's been my experience. My brothers and I were starting out back in Santa Ana in the early 1950s; we had no clue where our lives would take us. We had been raised around music and we were always interested in hearing good music, which is why I think we ended up playing the music that we did. Our ears were always open. The radio was so important to us back then, and if you walked around our neighborhood in Santa Ana, a lot of times you would hear songs come out of cars and people's windows. We didn't have a lot back then as far as money or anything like that. But we had our instruments[, and] we had a lot of dreams. I think the most important thing we did was to keep an open mind and try [to] absorb as much music as we could no matter where it came from.*
>
> *We were always up for hearing new little lyrics and learning new cords [sic] and things. I remember thinking on that first Beatles tour, when George Harrison was asking me about certain chords I was playing and how [I was] doing it, that I hadn't really done anything special except listen, learn*

and trample my own spin on things. That was never a big deal to me. I was just focused on trying to be as good a guitar player as I could be.

Traveling with the Righteous Brothers and playing with the Beatles, playing with Ray Charles and so many other great musicians were experiences I'll never forget. But a lot of it really comes down to our upbringing in Orange County and just how our neighborhood was the perfect place to grow up wanting to be a musician. We were surrounded by lots of good people, and while I think Orange County [is] still a great place, back then it was really something special. There were lots of neighborhoods and growing up in Santa Ana was a far more urban experience [than growing up in] *many other places in the county. We weren't near the beach or open fields. But being in a city I think help*[ed] *us hear more music and learn more music, and that really came in handy.*

I started out playing in Orange County, and here I am still playing in Orange County, which I am very happy about. People still come up to me and remember the old days, and as much as I like to remember stories, it's fun to hear other people's stories, too. The music in Orange County [affected] *a lot of people and still does. I'm still trying to learn new things on the guitar and come up with interesting ways to play. That never really gets out of your system, I don't think, no matter how old you get. Back then, I did it in Santa Ana, and today, I do it in Huntington Beach and other places. But I'm still doing it. I'm still an Orange County musician, and I'll always be very proud of that.*

TEN ROCK 'N' ROLL RESTING PLACES IN ORANGE COUNTY

KEVIN DUBROW

Pacific View Memorial Park, Corona Del Mar

He was the wild-eyed screamer from the very first number-one heavy metal band in the world, Quiet Riot. Born in Hollywood on October 29, 1955, Kevin DuBrow started out in the industry not as a singer but rather as a photographer. But once he met guitarist Randy Rhoads, things changed and changed fast. Competing with Van Halen throughout the Los Angeles club scene, his band Quiet Riot's knack for creating simple and effective metal anthems was established right up front. Once Randy Rhoads left to join Ozzy Osbourne in 1979, though, it changed the future of the band. For one thing, the name of the band simply became "DuBrow." Eventually though, they would reclaim the original band name and recruit Carlos Cavazos, bassist Rudy Sarzo and drummer Frankie Benali to form the most famous version of the band. Crafting a sound that relied as much on pop hooks as it did heavy metal riffs, the band released the album *Metal Health* in 1983, and by the end of the year, it had claimed the number-one spot on the charts. No metal band had never done that before, and it quickly ushered in a new age for commercial metal bands. All of a sudden, metal was hot. Dubrow's cocaine use and his big mouth equally got the band in trouble, and within several years, despite a popular follow-up to *Metal Health* called *Condition Critical*, the band found itself in meltdown mode.

But by the early 1990s, Dubrow's band mates had patched things up and gotten back to work. Throughout the '90s, they would tour and record in various incarnations, slowly but surely reclaiming the massive metal audience they left behind in the 1980s. Could there have been bands like Ratt, Cinderella and Poison without Quiet Riot? It's not likely. Tragically, on November 26, 2007, the news was released that Kevin DuBrow had died a week earlier in Las Vegas from an accidental cocaine overdose. Several years later, drummer Frankie Benali crafted a new version of the band, which to date continues touring and recording. However, there is not one show were Banali does not come out front and talk about his musical brother and band mate Kevin DuBrow, whose legacy as a microphone twirling madman and hyper energetic performer no doubt influenced many who came after him.

Quiet Riot was one of the first metal bands to gain massive popularity on MTV, and much of its success was the result of the crazily enthusiastic yet always fun and engaging personality of the lead singer. He may have burned many bridges over the years by badmouthing other bands and pounding his chest, but the legacy he left is an important one, and again, he was in part responsible for smashing down the doors that allowed so many other metal bands to find fame and fortune.

EDDIE COCHRAN

Forest Lawn Memorial Park, Cypress

He died at just twenty-one years old yet still managed to leave a mark as a true rock 'n' roll pioneer. Born in Minnesota, Eddie Cochran was raised in Oklahoma before moving to California with his family when he started his musical career in 1954. Cochran was one of rock's first guitar heroes. Before Pete Townsend, Jimmy Page or even Jimi Hendrix, there was Eddie Cochran.

His songs brilliantly identified teenage angst and sexual desire as suitable song subjects, and as result, he connected with a huge audience. "Summertime Blues," "20 Flight Rock," "Something Else," "C'mon Everybody"—these were the songs of a generation. He sounded tough, and he dressed flashy on stage, truly epitomizing the role of a 1950s rebel rocker. He originally got his break when a movie producer had him appear in the film *The Girl Can't Help It*, which also featured his version of "20 Flight Rock." That same year, he signed with Liberty Records, and the rest is history.

Although he only released one album during his lifetime, that didn't stop Cochran from being inducted into the Rock and Roll Hall of Fame and with good reason. He was just that profound. He was killed on April 17, 1960, after the taxi in which he was a passenger crashed on the way to a London airport at the end of one of his British tours. Rocker Gene Vincent and Cochran's fiancée, Sharon Seeley, were also injured in the crash. Interestingly, Shealy was a songwriter who had written Rick Nelson's number-one smash hit "Poor Little Fool." Vincent broke his leg in the crash and, as a result, had a limp for the rest of his life. Ironically, just before his death, Cochran released "Three Steps to Heaven." He may not be as famous today as his counterparts Buddy Holly, Rick Nelson or Gene Vincent, but that's probably only because of how young he was when he died.

Listen to his music today, and the rock 'n' roll rebellion played with a rockabilly verve is more than evident. Today, his legacy is probably larger in Britain than it is in the United States, which is probably because the UK is where Cochran died. That tragedy still resonates over there, and hopefully someday, the United States will embrace Cochran's legacy as forcefully as those around the world. As Peter Townshend said, "Eddie Cochran was a primal influence on me. He had a short career, and therefore so few songs, but his acoustic guitar playing was seminal—we played Eddie Cochran. It was all rooted in the blues of course, to some extent, but Eddie is my main man and always will be."

BRADLEY JAMES NOWELL

Westminster Memorial Park, Westminster

He'd recently been married, just become a father and his band was on the verge of releasing its major-label debut. That's when Bradley James Nowell, the founder, lead vocalist and guitarist of the band Sublime, died from a heroin overdose. His death occurred on May 25, 1996, and he was just twenty-eight years old. The death occurred at the Oceanview Motel in San

Francisco, where the band had just begun a short northern California tour to be followed by a trip to Europe and then a tour along the East Coast of the United States.

Born and raised in Long Beach, California, Nowell co-founded the band in 1988, along with drummer Bud Gaugh and bassist Eric Wilson. From the beginning, their sound incorporated many elements including ska, funk rap and pop. They also had been heavily influenced by the 1980s and '90s rap scene in Los Angeles and New York, pulling styles from many bands, including Public Enemy, NWA and the Beastie Boys. The bass-driven groups and island-style reggae rhythms proved an immediate hit with many people who saw the band play. They played at many parties and in backyards and released an independent album called *40 Ounces to Freedom* in 1992. In 1994, *Robbin' the Hood* came out, and the song "Date Rape," which was released in 1995, garnered a lot of airplay on Southern California's radio station KROQ. Given the amount of buzz surrounding the band, it was soon signed to MCA Records, and all of a sudden, the future looked bright for Sublime. The band's self-titled debut would become a huge mainstream success, going six times multiplatinum and influencing many bands around the world. But Nowell never got a chance to savor any of the success.

After his untimely death, Novell was cremated, and his ashes were distributed over one of his favorite coastline areas near Surfside, California. However, a headstone was placed at Westminster Memorial in Orange County in his memory.

Although the band broke up shortly after Nowell's death, in 2009, it began performing again with singer and guitar player Rome Ramirez fronting the band. The collaboration became known as Sublime with Rome.

BOBBY HATFIELD

Pacific View Memorial Park, Corona Del Mar

Better known as one of the Righteous Brothers, Bobbie Hatfield was born on August 10, 1940, in Beaver Dam, Wisconsin. As a young child, Hatfield's family moved to Anaheim, where he would sing in the choir and play baseball at Anaheim Union High School. Despite being a talented player considering a professional career, Hatfield decided to pursue a career in music.

EPILOGUE

After graduating from high school, Bobby Hatfield attended California State University–Long Beach, where he would meet his future singing partner Bill Medley. The two began performing as a duo in 1962 while in a band called the Paramours. Many fans noted the duo's similarity to African American vocal groups, and after one fan complimented them by saying, "That's righteous, brothers," they adopted the name that they would achieve fame with.

After a string of early hits, such as "Little Latin Lupe Lu," the Righteous Brothers teamed up with producer Phil Spector in 1964 for the number-one song "You've Lost That Lovin' Feelin'." This song, which featured an unknown Cher on backing vocals, received more radio airplay than any other song during the twentieth century.

The success of the Righteous Brothers continued throughout the next several years with another number-one single, "(You're My) Soul and Inspiration." However, as the decade came to a close and their success declined, the Righteous Brothers split up in 1968; Hatfield continued to tour under the Righteous Brothers' name, but success was limited.

After six years apart, the duo reunited for *The Sonny and Cher Comedy Hour* and had several fairly successful hits over the next several years. However, it would not be until the song "Unchained Melody" was used in the 1990 film *Ghost* that the Righteous Brothers would be back in the limelight.

In 2003, the Righteous Brothers were inducted into the Rock and Roll Hall of Fame by longtime admirer Billy Joel. A television special followed several years later in 2008.

During the early part of his career, Bobby Hatfield was briefly married to Joy Ciro, a dancer on the *T.A.M.I. Show*, during which time he had two children: Kalin and Bobby Jr. He married his second wife, Linda, in 1979, and fathered two more children: Vallyn and Dustin. Linda Hatfield passed away in 2010.

On November 5, 2003, hours before the Righteous Brothers were scheduled to perform in Kalamazoo, Michigan, Bobby Hatfield died in his sleep at the Radisson Hotel. A toxicology report showed that he had overdosed on cocaine in addition to having advanced coronary disease that had already caused a significant amount of blockage.

At the time of his death, Hatfield had lived in Newport Beach for over thirty years. His memorial service was held in Irvine, and he was buried at Pacific View Cemetery in his hometown of Newport Beach.

Epilogue

Sandy West

Forest Lawn Memorial Park, Cypress

She was the drummer and co-founder of the Runaways and was born in Long Beach on July 10, 1959. It was while living in Huntington Beach that she first began playing drums at the age of nine.

In late 1975, Sandy West was given Joan Jett's phone number by producer Kim Fowley. After an initial meeting, Jett and West were soon assisted by Fowley in finding other girls for their band. After several lineup changes, Cherie Currie, Lita Ford and Jackie Fox completed the band's core members.

Although together from only 1975 to 1979, and never experiencing much mainstream success, the Runaways were an extremely influential band and helped break new ground for female rockers. Their debut self-titled album in particular was praised for its raw style and proficient playing.

On this first album, as well as subsequent releases, West shared the writing credit on some songs with her fellow band members, although she was never responsible for the group's most successful songs, such as "Cherry Bomb" and "Queens of Noise."

Following the band's breakup, West attempted to start a new project with Lita Ford. When the new band quickly fell through, she was left to start the Sandy West Band. However, West would never go on to see the mainstream success of Ford or Jett, and her solo band only released one extended play.

Her drug and alcohol addictions plagued her for much of her life, and apart from a one-off reunion show with Currie and Fox in 1994, she never found much success in music. She toured California for much of the 1980s and 1990s, became a drum teacher and played with the Who's John Entwistle at various times. Sources say she often pined for a full Runaways tour, hoping to capitalize on the fame of her younger days.

In 2005, after years of struggling to make ends meet, West was diagnosed with lung cancer. Despite numerous treatments, she passed away in October 2006. A memorial tribute concert was later held in Los Angeles, featuring former Runaways band mate Cherie Currie. She was buried in Forest Lawn Memorial Park in Cypress, not far from where she grew up.

In 2010, a film adaptation of the band's career, simply titled *The Runaways*, was released. Sandy West was portrayed by actress Stella Maeve, who starred alongside Dakota Fanning and Kristen Stewart. The film was both a commercial and critical success.

DANIEL FLORES

Forest Lawn Memorial Park, Cypress

In 1929, Daniel Flores was born to Mexican field workers in Santa Paula, California. His fame would not come, however, until the late 1950s. In 1957, Challenge Records, owned by Gene Autry, signed a rockabilly singer named Dave Burgess. Not having produced a hit single, Burgess assembled a band in Hollywood on December 23, 1957.

The band, which featured Burgess on guitar, also featured Danny Flores on saxophone. Although the band had simply been assembled by studio executives to record a B-side for Burgess's "Train to Nowhere," they recorded an instrumental jam that Flores had written.

"Tequila," as Flores's song was known, quickly began receiving accolades. It hit number one in three weeks and went on to win a Grammy Award in 1959 (the first rock 'n' roll song to do so). Although many people know Flores's trademark "dirty sax" solo on the song, few realize that he is also the man who yells "Tequila!" three times throughout the track. Because of a contract with another recording studio, he was credited as "Chuck Rio" on the release.

Following the release of the song, which was recorded in three takes, the band that Challenge Records had put together began playing together under the name the Champs. "Tequila" was recorded by countless other artists and has been featured in numerous movies and television shows. Over fifty years after its release, it remains an enduring song that is still instantly recognizable to millions.

Flores died in 2006 in Huntington Beach after falling ill with pneumonia. Until the time of his death, he retained the worldwide rights to the song, although he signed away the rights within the United States. He was known to many as the "Godfather of Latino Rock" and continued performing well into old age. He is buried at Forest Lawn Memorial Park in Cypress.

JIMMY SULLIVAN

The Good Shepherd Cemetery, Huntington Beach

Born on February 9, 1981, James Owen Sullivan (better known as "The Rev") was the drummer and founding member of the Huntington Beach–

based heavy metal band Avenged Sevenfold. His father, Joe, recalled that from a young age, "he was desperately into music…in the bathtub when he was tiny he'd be banging away on things. Then, pots and pans—anything and everything."

His main influences when he was young ranged from Metallica to Dream Theater to Pantera, which coincided with his first serious drum kit at the age of ten. It was while attending school in Huntington Beach that he met the four other members of Avenged Sevenfold—M. Shadows, vocals; Zacky Vengeance, guitar; Synyster Gates, guitar; and Johnny Christ, bass.

The band's first release, *Sounding the Seventh Trumpet*, failed to attract much attention, but its sophomore album, *Waking the Fallen*, was both critically and commercially a success. The band was skyrocketed into stardom, however, with its 2005 LP *City of Evil*.

Their popularity only grew from there, with 2007's *Avenged Sevenfold* being named *Kerrang!* magazine's best album of the year. The band performed with such legends as Metallica, sold out world tours and quickly became one of the most prominent heavy metal bands in the world.

While working on the band's fifth full-length, Jimmy Sullivan was found dead in his Huntington Beach home on December 28, 2009. An autopsy performed two days later was inconclusive, but toxicology results revealed to the public in June that he died from an overdose of Oxycodone, Valium, alcohol and other substances. An enlarged heart was also found to have contributed to his death.

The band's fifth album, *Nightmare*, featured Mike Portnoy (one of Jimmy's idols) of Dream Theater on drums. The lyrical content of the album revolved around his passing and featured Sullivan's vocals on the song "Fiction," recorded just days before his death. Embracing Jimmy's legacy, the band has continued to grow, with both *Nightmare* and its follow up, *Hail to the King*, reaching the top of the *Billboard* charts.

Fans can still hear Jimmy's drumming on Avenged Sevenfold's first four albums, and his background vocals are prominently heard on such songs as "A Little Piece of Heaven," "Afterlife" and "Critical Acclaim." He is buried not far from his childhood home.

Epilogue

KAREN CARPENTER

Forest Lawn Memorial Cemetery, Cypress

Karen Carpenter was born in New Haven, Connecticut, but in the early 1960s, she moved with her family to Downey, California. In 1966, she and her brother, Richard, won a battle of the bands at the Hollywood Bowl, which landed them a recording contract. Nothing ever came of that, however, and it wasn't until 1969 that the Carpenters, after shopping a demo with several of their songs on it, got a contract from A&M Records.

Karen and Richard Carpenter would go on to become one of the most successful groups of the early 1970s, with Karen on the drums and singing lead vocals and Richard on the piano and providing backup vocals. Songs like "Close to You, "We've Only Just Begun" and "Rainy Days and Mondays" remain pop staples to this day. After winning three Grammy Awards, they eventually had their own television variety show.

Tragically, Karen developed depression and an eating disorder, and in February 1983, while at her parents' house in Downey sorting through some old clothes, she collapsed from cardiac arrest. Doctors soon determined that her longtime battle with anorexia had weakened her heart to the point that it could not go on. She was just thirty-two years old.

Originally, Carpenter was interred in Orange County at Forest Lawn Cypress Cemetery in Cyprus. However, in 2003, her remains were moved to a new location in the Pierce Brothers Valley Oaks Memorial Park. However, at the Sea Breeze Pet Cemetery in Huntington Beach, Richard and Karen Carpenter's German shepherds are laid to rest.

PAMELA COURSON

Fairhaven Memorial Park, Santa Ana

Born December 22, 1946, in Weed, California, Pamela Courson would go on to be best known as the longtime companion of Jim Morrison. As a child, she was shy and reclusive, and by junior high school, she was often truant. In high school, her family moved to Orange County, where she attended Orange Union High. She then left for Los Angeles and rented an apartment with her friend.

EPILOGUE

There exist multiple accounts of how Pamela Courson and Jim Morrison met in 1965. The most commonly accepted source states that it was at a Sunset Strip nightclub called the London Fog, while Courson was an art student at Los Angeles City College. Doors keyboardist Ray Manzarek recalled that Courson did indeed see the band at the London Fog, but it was Arthur Lee of Love who was interested in her first. It was Lee who would make Elektra Records aware of the Doors.

By all accounts, the relationship between Courson and Morrison was tumultuous. Fights and arguments between the two were numerous, and both had affairs outside their relationship.

However, their relationship would be cut short on July 3, 1971, when Courson found Morrison dead in the bathtub of their Parisian apartment. While the coroner listed his cause of death as heart failure, no formal autopsy was conducted, and there still exist many questions about the circumstances surrounding his death.

There also existed many questions regarding the state of Courson and Morrison's relationship. While Morrison's will said that he was unmarried, he named Courson as his heir and left his entire fortune to her. Legal battles would persist for years regarding his estate.

After Morrison's death, Courson broke off contact with the three remaining members of the Doors and returned to Los Angeles. She became a heroin-addled recluse, and some say that she even resorted to prostitution to fund her drug addiction.

It was on April 25, 1974, not even three years after Morrison's death, that Courson succumbed to her addiction. She died in her Los Angeles apartment of a heroin overdose, but before her death, she had spoken to neighbors about seeing Jim again soon, suggesting that she knew the end was near.

Initially it was Courson's wish to be buried with Jim in Paris, but due to legal complications, she was interred at Fairhaven Memorial Park in Santa Ana, not far from where she attended high school. Her grave reads "Pamela Susan Morrison," even though her name was never legally changed.

Courson's parents inherited the Morrison estate, although this led to a legal battle with Jim Morrison's parents for several years. Courson's family argued to the State of California that Courson and Morrison were legally married under Colorado's common-law marriage statute (Colorado was one of eleven states at the time that still had such a law). The court sided with Courson's parents, and they retained the rights to most of Morrison's estate.

LEO FENDER

Fairhaven Memorial Park, Santa Ana

Leo Fender was born near Anaheim in Orange County on August 10, 1909. An electronics enthusiast and radio repairman, he got involved with guitars after customers kept bringing him their external pickups that needed repairs. Before Fender got into the business, guitar players would amplify their instruments simply by attaching pickups to the surface of their hollow bodied guitars. What Fender figured out how to do was design and market an instrument that became the first successful solid-body guitar.

Over the years, Fender would go on to design many world-renowned guitars that became the favored models of such virtuosos as Eric Clapton, Keith Richards, Jimi Hendrix, Jeff Beck and Stevie Ray Vaughn. And he did so all from his Orange County plant located in Fullerton, not far from where he was born.

Leo Fender passed away on March 21, 1991. He suffered from Parkinson's disease for a number of years. At the time of his death, he was working on a guitar. Today, at the Fullerton Museum in Fullerton, California, there is a permanent exhibit in honor of the musical legend.

AFTERWORD

WITH JIM WASHBURN

Jim Washburn has covered music and popular culture for the *Orange County Register*, *Los Angeles Times*, *OC Weekly* and other publications. He is the coauthor of two books, including a history of Martin Guitars and has curated several museum exhibits. His merit badge requirements include running a record store, being a roadie, being a radio DJ, public speaking and playing the role of Mr. Peanut at a supermarket grand reopening.

When I was growing up, I never really thought about the music that actually came out of Orange County where I lived. It was later, after I learned about the Chantays being from Orange County, that I got impressed. Or the Righteous Brothers. I heard all of those records on the radio growing up, but I had no idea that this is where they came from.

In the 1960s, Orange County was perceived as a very right wing, John Birch Society bedroom community, which was all true to a point. But in some ways, that didn't work against music. I remember this congressman here back then talking about how rock 'n' roll was a communist plot, but a lot of people still thought that if kids could find a way to turn a buck while playing music, then great. If you could make some money, that's what it was about and so in that sense Orange County was even kind of inviting in terms of making music. The turning point was Vietnam in the late 1960s, when it became more of an "Us versus Them" situation and when the antiwar movement became more expressed in music. That's when Orange County became a lot more repressive, at least musically. It became very hard to get booked in places, and that changed things a great deal.

But then things loosened up when everyone realized how much money there was to be made, and that's when we started getting a lot of great national acts coming to play at the Anaheim Convention Center. The very first show I saw in Orange County was there, and it was Cream, with Spirit opening up. Cream was good, but I fell in love with Spirit and saw them a bunch of other times in Orange County, especially at the Golden Bear. I remember seeing Led Zeppelin at the Convention Center when I was about thirteen years old. I was there with a friend and we were looking very closely at what the guys were playing, noticing the Echo-plex that Jimmy Page had with the acoustic 360 that John Paul Jones was playing. This girl in front of us turned around and said, "You guys are like two little encyclopedias." I thought she was saying we were cool. Later on I realized it was the exact opposite.

When the punk thing started to happen in Orange County [in the] early 1970s, it didn't really work for me. With a lot of the bands, I felt like once you heard one song, you'd heard every song. So I was never really that into a lot of the bands around here that were classified as "punk." Around that time, I was more interested in Elvis Costello, the Blasters, X and bands like that, that while part of what was called the "punk" movement, were just, I felt, better bands.

I've seen a lot of great shows in Orange County over the years at some special venues like Linda's Doll Hut in Anaheim and Safari Sam's in Huntington Beach. One show at Sam's really stands out. I got them to book Jonathan Richman, and this was also when Ted Hawkins was an absolute unknown. He would be signed five years later and called the "Next Sam Cooke," but back then, he was a struggling street musician in Venice. Jonathan liked him, as did I, and so he opened up the series of four shows. Ted had never played before a sit-down audience. Jonathan encouraged him, and he got up there and did his songs about being broke and homeless—people were in tears. I get tears just thinking about it.

Who really knows if the world would be any different if no music had ever come out of Orange County? But then again, when you think of the simple fact of the Rillera brothers playing at Disneyland in the early '60s and thousands of kids hearing live electric guitar for the first time, who knows how many of those kids ran home and got out the Sears catalogue to buy a guitar?

INDEX

ABOUT THE AUTHOR

Chris Epting is an award-winning music and travel journalist and author of more than twenty pop-culture books, including *Led Zeppelin Crashed Here: The Locations of America's Rock and Roll Landmarks*, *Roadside Baseball* and *James Dean Died Here*. He writes extensively about music for a variety of outlets, including *Loudwire* and *Ultimate Classic Rock*. He recently completed writing a memoir with Phil Collen from Def Leppard and, as of this writing, is starting a new memoir project with singer/songwriter John Oates. Originally from New York, Chris lives in Huntington Beach with his wife and two children. Visit www.chrisepting.com for more information, or follow Chris on Twitter: @chrisepting.

Visit us at
www.historypress.net

This title is also available as an e-book